MOONLIGHT

HARRY R. BALLINGER

PAINTING SEA and SHORE

A Complete Guide to the Technique of Marine Painting in Oils

Watson-Guptill Publications   New York

Manufactured in the U.S.A.

ISBN 0–8230–3850–5

Library of Congress Catalog Card Number: 66–18664

First Printing, 1966
Second Printing, 1967
Third Printing, 1968
Fourth Printing, 1971
Fifth Printing, 1973

To Kay, who will always seem young and fair to me.

Contents

Introduction

As a rule, after I've finished a "How To Do It Book" on painting, I'm content to sit back and try to forget my literary efforts for at least a year or so. I have generally believed that it took me that long to convalesce from the arduous struggle of writing a book. After each book I'm always firmly convinced that writing should be left to professional writers and that artists should stick to their paint and brushes. It's a good idea but I find that someone is always twisting my arm to persuade me to write another book.

TWO BOOKS COMBINED

When I returned from a sketching and pleasure trip to Newfoundland this fall, I found a letter waiting for me from my esteemed publishers, Watson-Guptill, suggesting that we combine my first two books, *Painting Surf and Sea,* and *Painting Boats and Harbors*, forming one nice fat volume that would be a companion book to my recently published *Painting Landscapes.* After talking the matter over with my editor, Don Holden, I found that the idea appealed to me strongly and I ended up by enthusiastically agreeing to try to combine the text of both books into one volume, with the addition of some new information that was not included in the first two books. Actually it does make sense to have one new book cover the whole subject of marine painting. Anyone who likes to paint the sea usually likes to paint boats and harbors. In case you're not living near the seashore, a lake can be equally fascinating. I remember when I was living in Chicago years ago, that Lake Michigan could get good and rough and while there were no ground swells coming into shore, the waves breaking on the beach were as dramatic as anyone could wish.

UNDERSTANDING THE SEA

Almost everyone loves the sea and even non-painters seem to be fascinated by the sight of great waves breaking along the shore. It's a dramatic sight and one that never loses its appeal to the public. When it comes to painting a convincing surf scene, the painter should understand exactly what is happening in the constantly changing scene before him. A wave approaching the beach crests, bursts into foam, comes surging up the beach until it loses its momentum and then after levelling off is pulled back out to meet the next incoming wave. The action is so rapid that it's difficult to see it with the naked eye unless you know just what to look for. In this book the wave action is thoroughly explained by text—and many diagrams wherever necessary—so that when you are at the shore, you know what is happening and can easily identify the action taking place before you. Though there's a slight variation in the appearance of different waves, they all follow approximately the same basic pattern.

HARBORS

Harbor scenes have great charm and some people prefer them to ocean scenes. There is often some human interest that always appeals to everyone and a scene with boats, shacks, and wharfs often is more interesting to the average viewer than a seascape with only water and shore. I think that it's a fine idea to be able to paint all kinds of marine scenes, because it's a little monotonous to do only the sea. Boats and harbors are probably more difficult to paint than surf scenes because it's much harder to draw a boat than a wave. After all, moving water is not so difficult to paint when you understand the principles that govern its movement but boats have to be drawn correctly in order to look convincing. The artist has to understand their general contours and has to make them look as though they were in the water, not just sitting on top of it.

PAINTING OUTDOORS

It's very important to paint from nature if you really want to paint a convincing picture. After all, most of one's inspiration comes from nature. Even the non-representational painters admit using nature as the basis for many of their designs.

To be a marine painter takes quite a lot of stamina. It isn't quite as easy as painting flowers or a still life in a nice cozy studio. The weather isn't always ideal when you're working outdoors. On a day with a lot of surf, there's often a lot of wind which makes it a little difficult to keep the canvas from blowing away. Then the blowing spray fogs up your glasses if you're unfortunate enough to have to wear them, as I am. Occasionally the rising tide nearly washes you off the rock to which you're clinging. Then there's always the fun of trying to find shelter from the violent thunder shower under some overhanging ledge of rocks or in some small cave. I've found that no matter how far under the rocks you get, after you're there for awhile the cave ceiling always springs a leak which generally trickles right down the back of your neck.

Of course painting boats around a harbor isn't quite as strenuous; you can generally find some shelter from the elements either under a wharf or in some old shed. You'll find that almost any boat you'd like to paint has an unpleasant habit of putting to sea the minute you start to work on it. The tides are constantly rising or falling. A boat that looms majestically at the wharf when you start to paint it sometimes ends up in a deep hollow before you can finish it or else it completely disappears behind the wharf.

I hope that my random remarks about some of the hazards of outdoor painting won't discourage my readers and make them decide to go back to number painting again. Actually the fun of painting a good marine more than makes up for any inconveniences that you encounter along the way. The sea is the most exciting and dramatic subject in the world to paint. It can stimulate your imagination by being awe-inspiring one moment and breathtakingly beautiful the next. I've been painting the sea for thirty years and only wish I could spend another thirty years trying to do it justice.

I've tried to write this book in simple, non-technical language that can be readily understood by the amateur artist or student. I've avoided any fancy literary touches and have concentrated on practical information that I hope will help readers to paint some professional looking pictures of their own. In this book you will find chapters on the oil painting equipment that you will need, a great deal about design and composition which are the framework for all good pictures; chapters on perspective, color, and color mixings; also chapters on wave action and skies, painting surf on rocky shore, sandy beach, and open sea. Then there are chapters on drawing boats, planning and painting harbors. There will be many step-by-step painting demonstrations in color and in black and white showing the development of a painting from the first rough lay-in to the finished picture; also information about painting sea and harbor by day and by night, ships at sea and along the coast; some of my favorite harbors and some of my favorite coastal scenes, as well as creative painting in the studio and painting on location. Then there are ten marine drawings that can be used for practice paintings of your own.

Ever since I was a youngster, I have liked picture books, so you will find that this book has been profusely illustrated with quantities of paintings and drawings to further explain the text. Personally I'd rather look at pictures than wade through pages of print. If you feel as I do that a picture speaks louder than words, then this book should appeal to you. The editor has used for this book the same easy-to-read format used in *Painting Landscapes* which was admired so much when it was published last year. Then last but not least, you lucky people are getting two books for the price of one. This brilliant idea was suggested by my publishers, Watson-Guptill. I think that they have a point there but I hope you'll buy this book for the information about marine painting that it contains, rather than because it is a big bargain.

I've included in this book all the ideas that have helped me with my own painting over the years and I hope that they will help you with your own marine paintings.

HARRY R. BALLINGER
New Hartford, Connecticut

PATTERNS *In a harbor scene, the pattern of light and dark is usually established by the light sky and dark structures and reflections.*

1. Oil Painting Equipment

Although I've painted a great many watercolors in my life, I still consider oils a much easier and more flexible medium in which to work. The instructions in this book will be based on painting in oil, and I'll try to give you all the information at my disposal to help you handle this medium in a professional manner.

Some artists and many students think that they have to paint in watercolors for years before they acquire sufficient skill to work in oils. This assumption has always seemed absurd to me, for there is no medium as easy to work in as oil. You can make changes and repaint the picture with the greatest of ease if you're using oil, while in watercolor you're in trouble if a single wash goes wrong.

Painting in oil isn't like drawing with a pencil. Your brush strokes should be broad and strong, so accustom yourself to working on a fairly large scale from the start.

For the benefit of those who have had no previous experience with oil painting, I will list the necessary equipment for out-of-door painting.

SKETCHBOX

You'll need a sketchbox to carry your brushes and paints. A wooden box 12 x 16 inches is a good size, although you can use a 16 x 20 inch box if you prefer a more generous one. Sketchboxes are usually made of wood, though some people prefer those of aluminum because of their light weight. A smaller sketchbox is easier to carry, but I think one does better with a fairly generous size. Don't buy a fitted box. It contains a lot of useless colors and is much too expensive.

PALETTE

A palette comes with the sketchbox, though some artists like to use a paper palette with disposable sheets. If you use a wooden palette, it's a good idea to rub a little linseed oil on it, when new, in order to give it a smoother and less porous surface on which to mix your paint.

EASEL

You'll want a good, solid sketching easel of either wood or aluminum. My favorite is the Gloucester easel. It has a shelf-like arrangement below the canvas on which to rest the sketchbox and palette. This easel folds up compactly and has a shoulder strap for carrying. It's a great help when you're wandering around the docks with a sketchbox in one hand and a couple of canvases in the other. Some of the aluminum easels have a similar arrangement. If the easel hasn't a place

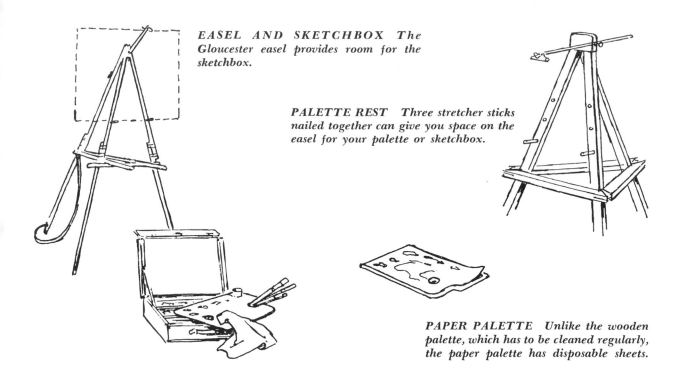

EASEL AND SKETCHBOX *The Gloucester easel provides room for the sketchbox.*

PALETTE REST *Three stretcher sticks nailed together can give you space on the easel for your palette or sketchbox.*

PAPER PALETTE *Unlike the wooden palette, which has to be cleaned regularly, the paper palette has disposable sheets.*

for a palette, you can nail three stretcher sticks together to fit down over the easel and give you a platform for it. I never paint while holding the palette in my left hand. It is uncomfortable and, moreover, you need your left hand to hold extra brushes or a paint rag.

BRUSHES

I recommend at least six brushes, ranging from a quarter of an inch to an inch in width, and I prefer bristle brushes to sable, because you're liable to get your work too polished with sable brushes. These brushes should be flat with a square end, either the type called *brights* with short bristles, or those with slightly longer bristles called *flats*.

It's a good idea to have two brushes of approximately the same size, one for light color and the other for dark—for your smaller ones, Nos. 2 and 3; for the next size, 4 and 5; and for the larger sizes, 7 and 8. For very fine lines you could buy a No. 1 brush, but you will be able to get a fairly fine line by using the side of your larger brushes and will rarely need a small brush. It's better always to use as large a brush as possible in order to cover your canvas rapidly and to keep your picture broad and simple.

OIL CUP AND KNIFE

14

You'll need a single oil cup about two inches in diameter and a palette knife of the trowel type, with the knife surface a little below the handle. This type of knife is easier to use than the straight type, and you get less paint on your hands.

COLORS

The list of colors in the Ballinger Palette is a simple one. It consists of ultramarine blue and cerulean blue, zinc white, cadmium yellow pale, cadmium orange,

BRUSHES *This is a rough drawing of two bristle brushes, one* **bright** *(short bristles) and one* flat *(long bristles).*

MEDIUM *Turpentine and linseed oil for thinning paint when you apply color to the canvas.*

OIL CUP AND KNIFE *You'll find this oil cup and trowel-like palette knife handy when you paint.*

cadmium red light, cadmium red medium or dark, and alizarin crimson. There are no earth colors—greens or black—in my palette.

These are the colors you'll employ most of the time. In addition, you can buy phthalo blue and viridian, though you will seldom use them.

MEDIUM AND VARNISH

Medium is the liquid you mix with your paint when you apply it to your canvas. I use a combination of linseed oil and turpentine, half and half. The oil should be a purified linseed oil, obtainable from any art materials store; any clear gum turpentine sold by paint stores is adequate. You'll also need retouching varnish. This is a light, quick-drying varnish to bring a gloss to the parts of the picture that look dull and lifeless. It can be sprayed on by a fixative blower or applied with a clean, soft brush if the painting is dry. You'll need only the retouch varnish when the picture dries out and you want to continue painting on it.

VIEW FINDER

One other useful piece of equipment is a view finder. This is simply a piece of cardboard with a rectangular opening in it and a wide enough border around the opening to blank out all but the scene that you are viewing. When you're sketching outdoors there's so much to see that it's often difficult to decide what to include in your picture and what to leave out. The view finder will help you isolate your projected composition.

CANVAS AND PANELS

The last item to consider is what to paint on. Canvas mounted on a cardboard panel is good because it's easy to transport. For larger sizes—20 x 24 inches or over—I would suggest a stretched canvas. Panels the size of your sketchbox are handy because you can carry them in the lid of your box, which has slots for

15

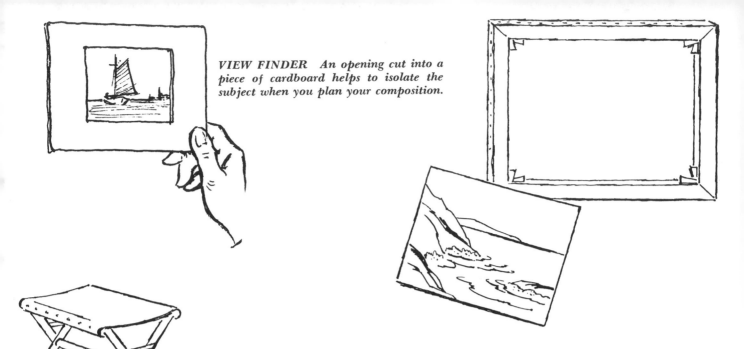

VIEW FINDER *An opening cut into a piece of cardboard helps to isolate the subject when you plan your composition.*

STOOL *When you paint outdoors, you may welcome this comfortable addition to your equipment.*

CANVAS AND PANELS *For smaller paintings, canvas mounted on cardboard is convenient. Stretched canvas is preferable for larger paintings.*

that purpose. Some of my friends use Masonite panels cut to a desired size. They are practically indestructible, but I don't like the surface—one side is too smooth and the other too rough.

ARTISTS' TERMS

At this point I'd like to list a few terms that artists use in describing pictures, which otherwise may be confusing to the beginner. Artists are constantly talking about *warm* and *cool* colors in their pictures. This means exactly what it says. The warm colors are red, yellow, orange, yellowish green, reddish purple and the browns or grays in which the warm colors predominate. The cool colors are the blues, bluish greens, blue-purples, and all the bluish grays.

By *value* we mean the degree of light and dark of any particular part of a picture or color. It also means the degree of light or dark of one color compared to another. *Tone* means about the same as value. *Halftones* are the values in a picture that are neither light nor shade—the values that are between the light and dark masses.

Key means the color value of the picture. A high-keyed painting would be one with light, bright colors, while a low-keyed picture would have dark, somber colors.

2. Composition

The first thing to consider in any picture is composition; that is, the dark and light pattern or design of the picture. Color alone won't make a good picture unless you also have a pleasing balance of the masses. I always try to think of every scene that I paint as a big, simple arrangement in two tones of light and dark. This is the framework for the whole picture. I try to see every portion of the picture either as part of the light or of the dark pattern. I always "tie" my darks together by having one dark spot blend into or overlap an adjoining one to make a large, irregular shape of dark rather than a number of isolated spots. Tie up the light spots in the same manner. The dark pattern, of course, makes the light one.

By thinking of the picture as a two-tone pattern of light and dark, you start with a simple poster-like arrangement. There is so much detail in nature that it's a great help to start a picture in simple masses and then, as you work along, modify some of the darks and lights, adding detail where necessary, only be careful not to lose your original simple design of light and dark.

TWO TONES **Plan your composition in two tones of light and dark.**

17

SIMPLE ARRANGEMENT *This harbor scene is a simple arrangement of light and dark tones.*

BALANCE IN COMPOSITION

There are a few standard forms of composition that are often used in the structural design of most pictures, but before we discuss them I'd like to explain what is meant by balance in a picture.

Pictures are composed on the principle of the steelyard balance. If this term is confusing, think of the old idea of the seesaw: an adult has to sit well in toward the center to be balanced by a child out on one end of the seesaw. Applied to a picture, a large mass of either light or dark near the center of your picture can be balanced by a small spot out near the edge.

PATTERNS OF LIGHT AND SHADE

It is easy to see a two-toned pattern of light and shade in a harbor scene on a bright day. As a rule, the sky and its reflection in the water will be part of the light pattern as will light pilothouses and the superstructure of the boats or those parts of buildings or wharfs that are in sunlight.

The darks will be in the hulls of the vessels, dark shadows under wharfs, reflections in the water and those parts of buildings and wharfs in shadow.

In a seascape, it's very easy to see a two-tone pattern of light and shade. Generally the white foam of the cresting waves and floating foam are part of your light pattern, also the sky and sometimes sunlit rocks or sand. The darks are of course the dark sea water and rocks in shadow, occasionally the sky if you're doing a storm or moonlight effect.

A popular type of composition is a light picture with balanced spots of dark. (See Composition No. 1.) Many pictures are painted with the same composition in reverse; that is, a dark picture with balanced light spots. (See Composition No. 2.) A moonlight scene with little light on the water and some of the foreground

18

NEWFOUNDLAND *There's a stark grandeur about the scenery in this distant spot that strongly appealed to me. The principal industry is fishing and the sturdy men of Newfoundland spend their whole lives in the age-old conflict of men against the sea.*

SCATTERED SPOTS of light and dark in a surf scene produce a scattered composition.

TYING UP   Tie up isolated spots of light into one large light pattern by having them blend or overlap one another. Do the same with the dark pattern.

20

SIMPLIFICATION *The composition in this boat scene is simplified into spots of light and dark, which still need to be integrated.*

TYING TOGETHER *The light and dark spots are "tied" together.*

foam with everything else in the picture dark would fit into this type of composition. So would the light boats and wharf in the upper left balanced by the rowboat in the lower right hand corner.

A composition with a dark base and a light upper portion is effective; so is the same in reverse—dark top and light lower portion. (See Composition Nos. 3 and 4.)

A pyramid composition with the weight and interest building up the middle is always strong and effective. (See Composition No. 5.)

There is also the L-shaped composition which builds up one side of the picture. (See Composition No. 6.)

I often use the S-shaped composition in which the interest swings through the picture from top to bottom like the shape of the letter S. It's always pleasing. (See Composition No. 7.)

21

FIRST STEP   Simplified patterns of light and dark.

*SECOND STEP   Light and dark tones are modified, values worked out,
but the over-all pattern is not lost.*

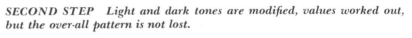

22

Sometimes the picture can be arranged in horizontal bands of alternate light and dark. (See Composition No 8.)

A circular design is good because it keeps the eye in the picture and concentrates attention on the center of interest. This same composition is sometimes called the *tunnel* because it uses the receding perspective lines and receding values to carry the eye deep into the picture to an opening at the end of the tunnel and sometimes the center of interest. (See Composition No. 9.)

The last compositional idea is the pattern which consists of a decorative arrangement of the lights and darks to form an interesting design throughout the picture. (See Composition No. 10.)

Often a combination of several of these compositions can be used in the same picture.

The difference between drawing and painting becomes apparent when you paint in masses of light and dark without any outline—when you draw you're working simply in line and outline with very few values. If you're able to get a fine decorative arrangement of your light and dark pattern in your painting, you'll automatically have a good picture. It will almost paint itself. But if the composition doesn't balance or work out with a decorative design no matter how much you struggle with it, the picture will never be any good. In that case there is nothing much left to do except shoot yourself or just give the whole thing up and start another picture somewhere else.

One way of learning about composition is to study every fine picture that you see and try to figure out what makes it good. Decide what kind of composition was used in its construction. By studying other paintings you can see how the principles of balance and composition which I've been discussing can be applied to your own picturemaking.

FIRST STEP In the harbor scene, the two-tone pattern is established.

23

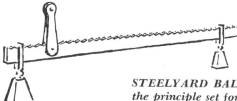

STEELYARD BALANCE *Balance in composition conforms to the principle set forth in this balance of weights.*

BALANCE OF SPOTS *The large spot in the center is balanced by the small one on the edge.*

BALANCE OF SPOTS *The large boat in the center is balanced by the small boat near the edge.*

PATTERNS   In a surf scene, the light pattern is the foam and sky, and the dark pattern is produced by the water and rocks.

COMPLETED PICTURE   The pattern is maintained even in the final painting.

26

COMPOSITION #1   This is a light picture with balanced spots of dark.

COMPOSITION #1   This is another example of balanced spots of dark in a light picture.

27

COMPOSITION #2 *The first composition is reversed; here's an example of a dark base with balanced spots of light.*

COMPOSITION #3 *Here is a picture with a dark base and a light dominating upper portion.*

28

COMPOSITION #4   Here the water is dark at the base, the land and sky are part of the light upper portion.

COMPOSITION #4   Here the water is light at the base, the land and sky are part of the dark upper portion.

29

COMPOSITION #5 *In a pyramid composition, the interest builds up the center of the composition.*

COMPOSITION #5   *Here's the same idea of a pyramid composition in a seascape.*

COMPOSITION #6   Interest building up the side of a picture produces the L-shaped composition.

COMPOSITION #6   The rocks along the sides of this seascape are another example of the L-shaped composition.

COMPOSITION #7 *The direction in this composition swings from top to bottom like the letter S.*

COMPOSITION #7 *The light pattern of the sky and the light foam pattern creates an over-all S-shaped composition.*

33

COMPOSITION #8 *A composition created by alternate bands of light and dark running horizontally across this picture.*

COMPOSITION #9 *The circular (tunnel) design carries the eye deep into the picture.*

34

COMPOSITION #10 *This scene of a fishing boat wrecked on a sandy beach is almost a sky picture. I was interested in the pattern of light in the sky and the reflected light on the wet sand. This is an example of circular composition.*

COMPOSITION #10 *I think there's something very sad about the sight of some fine old sailing vessels beached on a mud flat, never to sail the seas again.*

BRIAR NECK *Salt Island, between Gloucester and Rockport on Cape Ann, is connected with the mainland at low tide by a narrow strip of sand. However, the rest of the time it's a perfectly legitimate island. The warm sky reflects down into the entire picture; as you can see there are only a few cool touches in the painting. I think that offshore rocks or islands lend interest to a seascape, don't you?*

SURVIVAL *I don't know how the man on the raft made out, but he looks to me as though he was plenty tough and would survive.*

COMBINATION *Here I used a dark base with a pyramid composition.*

DRAWING AND PAINTING *These two drawings show (A) treatment of mass and (B) outline style.*

THE BUSY WATERFRONT *New York is a magic city, particularly around the harbor. I can watch the constant traffic all day long and never grow tired of the sight of ships sailing for faraway places.*

3. Perspective

Perspective plays an important part in any picture, so at this point I'd like to explain the general idea of perspective. There are two kinds of perspective, linear and aerial. Linear perspective concerns itself with the receding lines of all objects in the picture as these lines move back to the horizon line. Aerial perspective concerns itself with the effect of the atmosphere on the color and value of objects as they recede into the distance.

LINEAR PERSPECTIVE

The receding lines of all objects in a picture converge at a point on the horizon line at the level of your eye. Your eye level determines the horizon line. The eye line and the horizon line are the same. Everything above your eye level comes down, as it recedes, to the height of your eye on the horizon line; everything below comes up to it. A figure standing on a cliff sees a high horizon line, while a seated figure on a beach will see a low horizon.

Nearby objects below your eye line seem to tip down and have a more exaggerated perspective, which gradually flattens out as they go away from you up toward the horizon line. In linear perspective the lines of buildings also slant at a more extreme angle when they're close to you.

An easy way to understand perspective is to hold a thick book horizontally in front of you below your eye line. Note the amount of the top that you see, then gradually bring the book up to the level of your eye and see how the top flattens out until at the eye level the top is only a line.

In a marine painting linear perspective means that the waves would appear closer together and flatter as they near the horizon and, of course, much smaller. The same is true of lines above your eye level. Clouds become smaller and closer together as they near the horizon. In most marine scenes, the horizon line or your own eye line can be at any height that you desire. If you're doing a scene that's more or less panoramic, as though you were viewing the scene from a cliff, you would naturally have a high horizon line. When painting a harbor from an elevation, a hill or from the second story of a house, you could use a fairly high horizon line. In any seascape, a low horizon line will make any object like cliffs or foreground waves look a lot bigger. It would also make a boat in the foreground look more impressive. Usually it's better to use a horizon line at the level of a standing figure either on the shore or on a dock.

AERIAL PERSPECTIVE

In aerial perspective the colors and values of objects become paler and grayer as they recede toward the horizon line. There is always a certain amount of

THE SEINE BOAT *The old buildings on the wharfs at Gloucester were wonderfully picturesque to paint. Unfortunately, an energetic local firebug is gradually burning them all down. The new buildings being built to replace the old may be the last word in modern construction, but many of them are total losses from an artistic standpoint. The horizon line in this painting falls at the point where the water seems to be meeting the sky.*

HORIZON LINE The figure on the pier sees a higher horizon line than the figure in the boat.

HORIZON LINE The figure standing on the cliff sees a higher horizon line than the figure seated on the beach.

vapor or dust in the air that causes distant objects to be seen through a kind of haze, with the result that your light spots are a little darker in the distance and your dark spots a little grayer. The greater the space between an artist and an object, the more air you'll have to look through. To the painter the color of the air is the color of the sky. The distance of an object from the viewer can be suggested by the amount of sky color that the painter mixes with the local color of the object. The added sky color produces the effect of atmosphere and allows the different portions of the picture to appear at the right distance from the viewer. You can see the effect of atmosphere in a harbor scene. A brightly colored dory nearby will be more brilliant in color than one some distance out in the bay. A red house on a wharf would be grayer when seen from a distance. In the same way a line of distant cliffs will take on a blue-gray look instead of the local color of the rocks and vegetation.

To get the effect of plenty of distance in your picture, you can paint the foreground with bright color and stronger lights and darks, then you have the opportunity to gray your color and values as you go back into the picture. Sometimes it helps the effect of aerial perspective in your picture to pile on paint when painting the foreground and then painting the distant area more thinly. This idea has been used by a great many painters with gratifying success. Remember that aerial perspective influences the amount of detail you see in the distance. A boat at sea out near the horizon is just a spot while houses and wharfs across the bay can be painted as simple spots of light or dark.

43

STUDY PERSPECTIVE

If you wish to learn more about perspective there are a number of books available on the subject at most libraries. Try to get one that you can understand, if possible. I must admit that most of them seem rather complicated to me but if you stay with it and keep in mind the few simple ideas that I've listed above, I'm sure that you'll be able to work out the perspective in your picture without too much of a struggle.

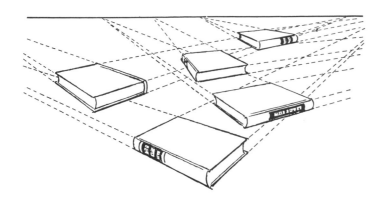

LINEAR PERSPECTIVE *By holding a thick book horizontally at three levels, you can see the laws of linear perspective in operation.*

THE ROCKY COAST *In this late afternoon scene, the low sunlight was coming from the right side of the picture. I decided to have the headland on that side cast a shadow across the center of the picture in order to concentrate the interest on the large wave in the foreground which was the center of interest. As we know from the study of aerial perspective, objects become grayer as they recede in the picture. The distant headland illustrates this point.*

MONHEGAN FOG *I like to paint fog scenes. Their mood of quiet mystery always appeals to me.*

MORNING HAZE *The large boats in this Gloucester scene were being refitted before going to sea again. As you can see the one on the right has her masts out. The over-all composition is a light scheme with dark spots.*

4. Color

I believe that it is better to use a simple selection of colors for your palette than to use every color under the sun. When you mix two colors to make a third, you get more sparkle and freshness than if you use a corresponding color right out of the tube. My choice of colors, which has been called the Ballinger Palette, is simply the standard high-keyed palette, with no green, purple or black and no earth colors.

MIXING YOUR COLORS

Before even attempting to paint, you have to learn to mix color. Until you learn to match the color that you see before you with your paints, you won't be able to paint anything the way it looks to you, for mixing a desired color is a matter of practice and study. I suggest that you spend some time trying to match in color and value every color in your living room. Try to match the color of the ceiling, walls, floor, draperies, and furniture. Match the general color of the carpet, for instance, both in the light and in the shadows. Try the same idea outdoors. Don't draw; just match the colors you see in front of you—the color of the grass, trees, houses, etc.

Most beginners can correctly identify a color that they see in front of them but are unable to combine the pigments on their palette in the proper proportions to produce the desired color.

There's one thing to remember: go gently when you're trying to mix a color; sometimes just a touch of color on the corner of your brush will be all you need. Compare the color that you're mixing with the color in front of you—put them side by side. If your color is too light, add more paint; if too dark, add white; if too warm, add more cool color. While it does take practice to match the exact color and tone that you see before you, it can be done with perseverance.

ARRANGING COLORS ON YOUR PALETTE

The colors should be arranged on your palette starting with the cool ones on the left, white next, then the warm ones, arranged in the order of the color wheel.
1   *Ultramarine blue.* This is a dark, purplish blue which, combined with red, can be used for strong darks. I use the blue to darken the color, then add cadmium red deep, cadmium red light or cadmium orange, depending on how warm a dark I desire. As a rule, I like to have my darks a little on the warm side to give them more richness and depth than if they were a cold blue or purple.
2   *Cerulean blue.* This is a paler, more greenish blue and makes lovely, pearly grays when combined with cadmium red light and white. If you desire more of a

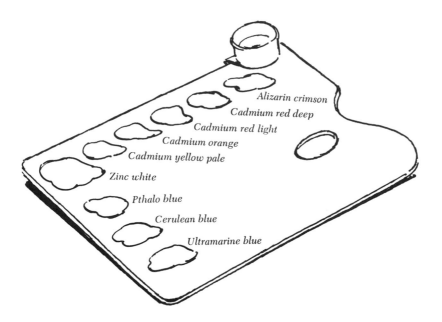

Alizarin crimson
Cadmium red deep
Cadmium red light
Cadmium orange
Cadmium yellow pale
Zinc white
Pthalo blue
Cerulean blue
Ultramarine blue

COLORS ON PALETTE *Set the colors on your palette in the same arrangement as the colors on the color wheel: from cool to warm.*

tan color, add a little cadmium orange to your gray mixture. However, don't add cadmium yellow pale, as this will immediately produce a greenish tint. Cerulean blue is a very useful color because it's already grayed up as it comes from the tube and can be used to gray up other colors or combinations of colors. It makes a fine light green when combined with cadmium yellow pale. For darker greens you can use ultramarine blue and cadmium yellow pale and for a very dark olive-green, use ultramarine blue with cadmium orange.

3 *Phthalo blue* and *viridian*. Once in a while you can use a little phthalo blue or viridian for some special spot, but I don't think you'll need either of them often. Phthalo blue is a powerful dye, like Prussian blue, and should be used with restraint. Sometimes a little mixed with white will make a strong, very light blue that can be used in painting a sky. For ordinary use it's too powerful for the other colors in your palette.

Viridian is a pleasant blue-green and is useful in painting parts of a cresting wave in a surf scene or the dark green in the quiet water of a harbor.

4 *Zinc white*. This should be fairly liquid so that it will mix readily with your colors and flow on easily. Of course you can use it to gray up your colors when you're mixing lighter hues, but don't mix too much white with your color because you're liable to give a chalky look to your painting. For instance, you can get light enough greens by using cadmium yellow pale with your blue, which is a nice light color, without using any white at all.

5 *Cadmium yellow pale* is like a lemon yellow. Be sure that they don't sell you cadmium yellow *light* at the art materials store, as this is a warmer color and doesn't work as well as cadmium yellow *pale*.

6 *Cadmium orange* is just about the warmest kind of yellow. By mixing different quantities of cadmium yellow pale and cadmium orange, you can get any degree of warmth that you desire in your yellows.

7 *Cadmium red light.* Be sure it's a bright orange-red, like vermilion.

8 *Cadmium red deep* or *medium.* Either of these is all right for use in your dark red or combined with ultramarine blue to make black.

9 *Alizarin crimson.* I prefer this to rose madder because it's a more permanent color. I use alizarin crimson only occasionally in a picture. In painting, as in life, there shouldn't be too many purple passages. However, there are some occasions when alizarin crimson is very effective. Diluted with white you can get some nice rose pinks; mixed with cadmium red light, it makes a strong and brilliant red.

COMBINING COLORS

Here in brief is the way to mix some of the colors you will use most often:

Black. Ultramarine blue and cadmium red deep, with just a touch of cadmium orange, will give the effect of black paint, but it will have more brilliance than black paint, which generally has a tendency to resemble shoe polish.

Darks. For dark reds or browns, use ultramarine blue with cadmium red deep or cadmium red light to warm it up. For browns, use a little orange and less of the blue. For dark blues, use less of the warm colors; for dark greens, ultramarine blue with cadmium orange and sometimes a little cadmium red light. Don't mix alizarin crimson with ultramarine blue unless you want to get a rip-roaring purple.

White. Use zinc white, of course, generally with just a touch of warm or cool color, because whites in nature are seldom exactly white.

Grays. Mix cerulean blue and cadmium red light with white.

Tan. Add a little orange to the above gray mixture.

Greens. For light greens, use cerulean blue and cadmium yellow pale; for darker greens, use ultramarine blue instead of cerulean. If you want a dark olive-green, use ultramarine blue combined with orange.

When you're mixing a color, try not to mix the paint too thoroughly on your palette. You'll have more color vibration, when you apply paint to the canvas, if it isn't overly blended. You'll get an effect of broken color which will give a sparkle to the picture.

AFTER THE PAINTING SESSION

Usually, when you finish a day's painting, you clean off only the center of your palette, leaving the gobs of color around the edges. They will usually stay fresh for several days, so the paint won't be wasted. If you use a disposable paper palette, you can transfer the piles of paint to a fresh sheet and throw away the old one.

When I finish the day's painting, I always place my brushes in a flat tin of kerosene with the handles resting on the edge of the pan and the bristles lying flat on the bottom of the pan. This is much better for the brushes than standing them upright in kerosene, which is liable to bend and distort the bristles.

49

When you want to use your brushes again, just wipe them off with a rag and they'll be ready for work. Every two or three weeks you can give them a real wash with brown laundry soap and water. Take care to rub the soap into the bristles right up to the ferrule of the brush so that no paint will harden in the bristles to spoil your brushes. Your brushes will last longer this way, as constant washing with soap and water is apt to wear them out. Too much washing of your brushes is also bad for your hands and your disposition, situations to avoid at all cost!

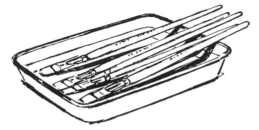

CLEANING BRUSHES *I place my brushes horizontally in a flat tin of kerosene. This method cleans the brushes without harming the bristles.*

5. Wave Action

The most important part of a marine painting is the water itself. Until you know just what changes a wave goes through when it breaks on shore, you can't even think about trying to paint a seascape.

WAVE MOVEMENT

In order to paint a surf scene convincingly, it's necessary to understand what is happening before your eyes. The surf moves so rapidly that it's hard to see the action unless you know exactly what to look for. Therefore, I will explain each step in the action of a wave from the time it approaches the shore until it spends its force against the shore and pours back out to sea as floating foam.

Waves move into shore in parallel lines from the open sea. They are evenly spaced, and crest as they get into shallow water at about the same spot each time.

A cross section of a wave approaching the shore is a triangle with the steepest side toward shore. As a wave reaches shallow water, the front plane toward shore gets steeper and steeper until finally the top of the wave collapses forward, rolls over and down, hitting the front slope of the wave near the base with a mighty rebound. The weight of the water behind it forces the foam on toward shore in a series of bouncing masses.

WAVE MOVEMENT   As they come in from the sea, waves move in roughly parallel lines, evenly spaced from one another. The waves in shallow water crest at about the same place each time.

Front View

Side View

UNCRESTED WAVE

WAVE STARTING TO CREST

CRESTING WAVE SHOWING WATER BACK OF FOAM

WAVE BREAKS INTO FOAM

FLATTENED-OUT WAVE MOVING INTO SHORE

END OF FORWARD MOVEMENT IN FLOATING FOAM

When the top of the wave rolls forward and over, and breaks into foam, there's briefly visible a sheet of water back of the foam that is almost immediately blown apart by the imprisoned air under it. Because of the foam and air bubbles underneath, this sheet of water is often a lovely, pale jade-green in color.

When the sheet of water at the top of the cresting wave disappears, there is left a large mass of foam that comes cascading down the front of the wave in terraces. As the wave moves on toward shore, it gradually flattens out and leaves a twisted mass of foam trailing out behind it. The wave gets flatter as it moves toward shore, though there is still weight and thickness to the mass of foam as long as the forward movement continues. When the wave has traveled up and over the rocks as far as its momentum will carry it, the foam then levels off and pours back down to the level of the sea, directly in front of the rocks.

WAVES ON ROCKS AND BEACH

Sometimes the mass of water pouring off the rocks is so heavy that it gives the effect of a flattened-out wave heading back out to sea. When this backwash hits an advancing wave, you sometimes get quite an impressive splash. Personally, I think it's confusing to play up the backwash too much in a picture. It rather detracts from the power that you get in your painting when you have all the waves moving in toward shore in the same general direction.

On a flat, sandy beach there's very little backwash noticeable. When the wave travels up the beach and reaches the end of its forward movement, it turns into floating foam and gradually moves out to sea again.

STUDY THE DRAWINGS

The drawings in this chapter show the action of a wave from the time it crests and moves into shore until it finally pours back out to sea again.

A wave crests at its highest point when it gets into shallow water. The foam spreads out toward each end of the wave. This action is especially easy to see when you watch surf on a sandy beach. There the waves, because of the uniform depth of the water, generally show a wide stretch of foam when cresting and the waves appear much longer from end to end than on a rocky shore with its varying depths of water.

When painting a breaking wave coming toward you, notice that the bottom edge of the foam tumbling down the face of the wave can be suggested by sweeping curves deeper at the middle and tapering out toward the ends of the wave. A profile view of a breaking wave suggests a series of terraces from the top to the bottom in a convex contour rather than the concave shape that some painters imagine a cresting wave assumes.

A wave doesn't really roll over completely when it crests; just the top portion rolls over and down. The foam then goes bouncing along toward shore, pushed along by the volume of water behind it and getting flatter and more spread out as it goes along. I always paint these masses of foam with up and down strokes of my brush across the action of the foam itself. The floating foam should be painted with horizontal strokes in the direction in which the foam is moving. This will make it lie flat on the surface of the water.

If you study the drawings on these pages, I think you can easily understand the system on which surf operates. There will be more about this in the chapters on Painting Surf on a Rocky Shore, and Painting Surf on a Sandy Beach.

53

WAVE MOVEMENT *This is a diagram of a cresting wave (front view). The wave crests at its highest point in shallow water.*

WAVE MOVEMENT *The bold line in this diagram suggests the bottom edge of the foam beneath a cresting wave: a curved line that deepens in the middle and tapers at the edges.*

FOAM   I use up and down brush strokes to suggest the mass of the foam in a wave that has weight and thickness, and horizontal brush strokes to suggest the floating foam as it flattens and disperses.

55

WAVE MOVEMENT   Only the top of a cresting wave rolls over.

6. Skies

In a painting, the sky is extremely important because it provides the key to the whole picture. Therefore, it should be painted first. It will be helpful to picture the sky as the interior of a great dome.

SKY AS A DOME

There is a layer of vapor over the surface of the earth which grays up distant objects. When you look straight up into the sky, instead of looking at an angle, you see the peak of the dome through the clearest air; that is, you're looking through the thinnest portion of the vapor layer, and consequently you see more of the true color of the sky.

Over the land this veil is a combination of dust and smoke. Over the sea it's vapor. In addition to graying up the distance, it sometimes reflects quite brilliant colors from the sun.

So you see, a cloudless sky isn't just blue all over. Its color is affected by the layers of vapor and by the sun. Directly overhead it is a darker, more intense blue which changes to a paler blue-green lower in the sky, until finally, near the horizon, it becomes a pinky lavender. Thus we see the sky appears darker overhead and lighter near the horizon. This gradation of color and tones gives the sky its domed effect.

The warm light from the sun also affects the color of the whole sky so that you'll find pink and pale orange modifying its blue tones.

When you're looking toward the sun, as you frequently do when painting a picture with back lighting, you'll find that the sky is extremely warm and glowing in color. The sky can then be painted in tones of warm pink and yellow with hardly any blue showing at all.

When I'm painting a picture with side lighting, I generally warm the sky as I get nearer the side from which the light is coming. Sometimes the sky opposite the sun will also receive warmth.

I believe it was Winslow Homer who disliked painting blue skies. I heartily agree with him; any color of the sky suits me as long as it isn't blue. A bright blue sky looks almost too "pretty," is reminiscent of calendar art. Fortunately, there is such a wide variety of skies to paint that, if you're lucky, you'll hardly ever have to paint a blue one.

CLOUDY SKY

A cloudy sky offers the artist a much better opportunity to compose a fine decorative arrangement of light and shade. A cloudy sky makes it possible to use cloud

THE GREEN WAVE This scene was painted at York Beach, Maine, one sunny afternoon. I tried to paint the pattern of the clouds in harmony with the movement of the sea. Although I'm not too fond of blue skies in a seascape, they're occasionally well worth painting. I think my only objection to blue skies is that they've been done so often that they're inclined to look rather like calendar art. However, if you paint the sea in many different moods, you'll probably come back to painting sunny blue skies with pleasure. I'm sure that the general public prefers them to any other kind of picture. So if you wish to sell every picture you paint, be sure to stick to blue skies.

STRATO-CUMULUS

ALTO-CUMULUS: MACKEREL SKY

CUMULUS

STRATUS

NIMBUS

CIRRUS

shadows throughout the picture, and you can concentrate your light and shade exactly where you want it. I personally think that cloud shadows are God's gift to the artist.

In order to paint clouds convincingly, it's necessary to study their formations. One may know the correct names for the different types of clouds; however, the important thing is to be able to draw them as they look and paint them in their proper color and value.

Clouds form and float at approximately three different levels; high, middle, and low. They have Latin names which make them sound more impressive. After spending three unhappy years studying first year Latin without much success, I finally decided to let the Latins mess around with their own language. Although I'm not much of a Latin scholar, here, at least, are the names of the main types of clouds:

The low clouds consist of: cumulus—the round woolly fair weather ones; stratus—a layer-like cloud lying quite low; and nimbus—a rain cloud.

You can have clouds that are a combination of two of these three types: cumulo-nimbus or thunderhead; nimbo-stratus or strato-cumulus, which cover most of the sky in a simple dark mass.

The middle level clouds are called alto. These can be alto-cumulus, which sometimes form a mackerel sky. Alto-stratus are layer-like clouds at a middle level.

The higher clouds are called cirrus and are inclined to be thin and wispy. There are cirro-stratus which are in layers or sheets, and cirro-cumulus which lie in ridges or ripples across the sky.

Even if you can't remember these fancy names for the clouds, try to remember the characteristic shapes of the important types.

When you're painting a cloudy sky, you'll notice that the clouds higher up in the sky, more nearly overhead, are brighter and have more color in them. They can be painted in more sweeping curves, while the clouds as they approach the horizon line become grayer and closer together in more horizontal lines. They, of course, become smaller the farther down they get, near the horizon. Just above the horizon, owing to the previously mentioned layer of vapor, the clouds disappear as individual masses. So there are no clouds just above the horizon; only one fairly light pinkish-blue tone.

The sky should sometimes be toned down a little so that it won't detract from the brilliance of the water or the foreground interest. This is always the case unless you are painting a sky picture with emphasis on the sky itself. In that case, the rest of the picture has to be toned down in order not to detract from the brilliance of the sky. You should have only one main center of interest in your picture.

CLOUD EDGES

When you're painting clouds, try to keep many of their edges rather soft and mushy. They have volume, light, and shade; yet they look as if they were made of vapor, not as though they were made of tin. I don't believe that anyone likes a picture in which the clouds appear to be riveted to the sky. Clouds should always have a general decorative pattern that will go with the lines of the rest of the picture. (See the painting entitled *The Green Wave*.)

DESIGN, MOVEMENT, AND COLOR

When I'm about to start painting a sky, I carefully study the design of the

CREW OF THE MARY LOU *The crew of a wrecked dragger was being picked up by another fishing boat. I used the idea of cloud shadows in order to paint the dory and crew in silhouette against the sunlit wave behind them.*

CLOUD SHADOWS *The large trawler and the shore on the right were in shadow while the small fishing boat in the foreground and the land on the left were in sunlight. Light skies with dark clouds are just about the easiest skies to paint.*

clouds. When I see an arrangement of their pattern of light and shade that I think would go with the rest of the picture, I quickly sketch it in before it can change.

As you know, clouds, though apparently standing still, are really moving all the time. It's necessary, therefore, if you like a certain effect, to sketch it in as rapidly as you can, because it will change completely in a few minutes.

I like to keep quite a little warmth in the shadows of the clouds, particularly those high overhead. As they get farther away and nearer the horizon, you can use a little less warmth.

Distance cools all colors, as well as graying them up. For example, warm pink rocks would be a lot cooler a quarter of a mile away than if they were in the immediate foreground.

Don't forget, while painting the sky, to watch its effect on the rest of the picture. When you have a dark leaden sky, you get a dark sea or harbor. On the other hand, a bright blue sky produces blue water. The sea is really like a mirror and picks up any changes in the sky.

You can see what happens when clouds cast shadows over parts of the scene, then you can make up your mind where you want your brilliant lights and what portions of your picture should be in shadow. Of course, the sky color reflects down over the whole picture.

We've all watched the rapid change that takes place in a harbor when a blue sky becomes overcast. The blue in the water of the harbor completely vanishes and is replaced by a leaden expanse that has picked up the color of the sky. I think the toughest thing about outdoor painting is to capture some such effect before it changes completely.

I remember starting a fascinating fog scene one morning at Gloucester, on Cape Ann. A fisherman was loading gear in a lobster boat tied up to a float with a little of the wharf seen in the distance. It looked mysterious and picturesque with a soft diffused down light on it, but by the time I had drawn it in, the fog had disappeared and I was left with a most unpleasant background, complete with gas tanks and brand new shiny-looking warehouses. The mystery was gone. There remained only a flat sunlight effect that came from behind me, obliterating all shadows. While I was deciding what to do, the lobsterman started up his motor and happily chugged away for some distant point outside the harbor, leaving behind a discouraged artist who felt like giving up the whole thing and turning to flower painting!

SKY TECHNIQUES

When painting clouds, use a large brush and paint as freely and loosely as possible with many soft edges. Paint quite a lot of sky with vertical brush strokes instead of horizontal ones. In this way you paint across the horizontal clouds and achieve a looser, more artistic effect, one that helps to suggest the domed look of the sky. When painting clouds, try to keep their shadows as simple as possible, with hardly any detail in them. The light areas should be simple with the highlights toward the center; that is, well inside the light areas of the clouds. You can suggest modeling, in the different masses, by the degree of sharpness or softness you give to their edges. Clouds have much softer edges than you would think possible. You can paint a whole sky with only one or two sharp touches, having all the rest of the edges simply melt into each other.

That is why masts or buildings with comparatively sharp edges are so effective when silhouetted against the soft, mushy clouds behind them.

If you're undecided whether an edge is sharp or soft, just squint at it for a moment with eyes half closed. The soft edges, when studied in this manner, will disappear. As a rule, the greater the contrast between two adjoining masses the sharper the edges; with less contrast, the softer the edges. If you think that the edge of a cloud is quite sharp, compare it to the mast or smokestack of a boat and you'll see that it's really fairly soft.

The easiest skies to paint are generally light skies with dark clouds, or fairly dark skies with white clouds. When trying to decide how light or how dark to paint the sky, compare it with the strongest lights or the darkest darks in your picture. You'll find that skies are usually fairly light in value unless they're dark storm clouds or you're painting a night scene.

CLOUDS Note the aerial perspective in the clouds. They become grayer, flatter, and smaller the closer they get to the horizon.

MAKING PORT *The reflected light on the water helps to direct our attention to the dragger in the middle distance which is our center of interest. Study where cloud shadows fall. This may help you plan out your light and dark patterns in the picture.*

CLOUD EDGES *You can suggest modeling in the different cloud masses by varying the degree of sharpness and softness of their edges. Vertical brush strokes were used in this sky.*

SKY VALUES   Here's a light sky with dark clouds.

SKY VALUES   Here's a dark sky with light clouds.

7. Planning a Seascape

When you go out to the shore to paint, look the scene over carefully and select the first view that looks as though it would make an interesting picture. Don't waste any time trying to find something better, because you may not find it. If the particular scene at which you are looking interests you, that's it.

STUDY THE SCENE

Study your scene from several different directions and try to find the angle that will give you the most pleasing arrangement of the areas of light and shade. Also carefully note the direction of the light and which way the sun is moving, so that your light effect won't change too drastically. It's also a good idea to have a schedule of the tides in the vicinity, so that you can tell whether the tide is rising or falling, and can plan your picture accordingly.

Study the scene for a few minutes and note where the oncoming waves crest; then pick a spot for your center of interest where a wave is really breaking and arrange the rest of the picture to go with it.

Before starting to paint, it will probably help if you make two or three pencil sketches to be sure that you have a good black-and-white design for your painting.

FIND CENTER OF INTEREST

Since the water is the most important part of a seascape, be sure you leave plenty of space for the surf and water; the action of the waves should be the first thing you plan. The foreground interest, with rocks or sandy beach, should be only of secondary importance.

Many students become so interested in drawing the foreground rocks or beach that they put off painting the surf until everything else in the picture is finished; then they find that they haven't any room for the surf.

If, for your center of interest, you decide to have a wave breaking near the middle of your picture, you may perhaps have room for a flattened-out wave pouring over rocks in the foreground. Out at sea you can show other uncrested waves moving in toward shore. A distant headland sometimes lends interest to your pictures.

Be sure that there's some kind of foreground interest to bring the foreground toward you and to give depth to the picture. You naturally see more detail near you so you must be sure to have something interesting to paint in the foreground.

Rocks in the foreground are always good as they have strong, decorative shapes that make a fine contrast with the light foam of the water. On a sandy beach,

67

NORTH ATLANTIC In this picture of the New England coast, the strongest lights are in the cresting wave and in the water pouring over the rocks. Toning down the value of the sky helped to concentrate the interest on the surf. I like to paint the water pouring off the foreground rocks. It only lasts a few seconds, but I think it looks good in a picture.

you can use the dark of the wet sand at the water's edge to give contrast and interest to the foreground; also any interesting details such as tidal pools in the sand, seaweed, driftwood, etc.

It's a good plan, when painting a seascape, to look along the beach and paint the scene at an angle rather than to look straight out to sea with surf coming right toward you. You can show action more easily by viewing the surf at an angle; you also get away from so many horizontal lines and have much more interesting perspective in your picture.

STUDY THE LIGHT

The direction of the light in your picture is very important. It's a good plan to paint a scene that has a side lighting or one that has the light coming from within the picture, producing a back lighting.

POINT OF VIEW *Painting a seascape from an angle is a good way to add interest to your surf scene.*

SIDE LIGHTING *A strong direction of light in the picture is a very important way to tie in the elements of your painting. Here the side lighting is from the right.*

BACK LIGHTING *Notice the many values achieved in the waves by using back lighting.*

70

Often a flat light over the whole picture is uninteresting and may spoil what might be a fine painting. Sometimes just a simple, diffused down light is effective; that's the kind of light you would get on overcast, foggy, or rainy days. You can't paint a picture unless you know exactly where the light is coming from; so be sure to figure out the direction of your light before you start to paint.

To summarize—when planning the picture, first find a view that appeals to you; then select the best painting angle from a composition standpoint. Familiarize yourself with the movement of the tides and be sure that the direction of the light will give you enough light and shade with which to work.

Painting by the sea is a tough job, because the ocean isn't at all cooperative and sometimes seems violently antagonistic. However, it's surely worth the trouble if you're able to capture some of the grandeur and beauty of the sea in your canvas. So think nothing of it if your canvas blows away or you get washed off a rock. To the marine painter, this is all good, clean fun.

DOWN LIGHTING   The effect of diffused light falling from above is ideal for foggy or stormy scenes. In a fog scene, you can use your whole value range from light to dark in the foreground. The rest of the picture can be grayed up as it recedes in the distance. I like the mystery of a fog scene with distant objects almost completely lost in the mist.

CLEARING As you can see in this picture of stormy weather at Monhegan Island, the waves coming into shore were deflected by the rocks in the center of the picture. This change of direction caused the waves to swing into the small opening in the rocks in the foreground, an effect which gives variety to the wave movement in the picture. The light breaking through the clouds and reflecting on the water helped to dramatize the scene. Collection, Mr. and Mrs. Spencer Lake.

8. Painting a Seascape

A marine is really a portrait of one nice big wave, with plenty of splash to it. Everything else in the picture should contribute to the importance of the wave which is your center of interest.

Sometimes you'll have your important wave surging over the foreground rocks or you'll feature the water pouring off rocks farther out to sea after the wave has rolled into shore. But mostly you'll feature a big wave cresting near the center of the picture and dashing against some centrally located rocks. A good moment to paint your important wave is just as the sheet of water at the top of the wave is disappearing and you have a large impressive mass of white foam tumbling down the front of the wave toward you.

As I mentioned in the preceding chapter, first pick out the spot that you wish to paint; study the scene carefully and note where the waves are really breaking. Next, decide on the action that will look best in your picture. Note the direction of the light and whether the tide is rising or falling. Then, decide just how much of the scene to include in your picture. It's a good plan to concentrate on the most interesting portion of the scene before you, rather than to try to paint a wide panorama. Generally, there's too much to see in the scene before you and you have enough information for several pictures. The view finder, as previously mentioned, often helps in deciding what portion of the scene to paint, as it automatically eliminates all of the scene except the particular part that you are studying.

PLANNING THE BLACK-AND-WHITE DESIGN

When starting to paint the picture, carefully draw in outline, with a little blue paint and lots of medium, the shapes of all the important masses of light and dark in the picture. The pattern of your picture will thus be clearly defined. Be sure to draw the shapes of the white foam areas of your cresting waves and floating foam, as well as the shapes of the rocks and any of the cloud formations in the sky.

PLANNING THE COLORS

When you've decided on the black-and-white design of your picture, then you must study the color scheme of the scene in front of you.

So far in this book, I have talked more about values and the light and dark pattern of a picture than I have about color. I've done this because I consider that tone and value are the very framework of your picture. If you haven't a

73

VIEW FINDER Isolating portions of the scene with a finder helps you to compose your seascape. By using the view finder, you can find a variety of interesting compositions in different portions of the same picture.

HAZY DAY Coordinate the action of the waves with the general movement of the whole mass of water. In this picture of the surf rolling in on a rocky shore, I tried to suggest a misty day with a warm glow over the whole painting. I used rather strong highlights on the rocks in the foreground to make them look wet. Collection, William Matt.

good black-and-white pattern to your picture, you haven't a good picture. However, color is extremely important and should always be carefully considered.

It's a fine idea to have imagination and to be able to change everything around in your picture to suit yourself. But I think you'll learn more about marine painting if at first you honestly try to paint the scene before you just exactly the way it looks. By painting just what you see in a literal manner, you gain a lot of valuable information about the surf and shore that will be a great help to you later on when you want to paint a picture in the studio. After all, you can't even start to paint a picture until you've learned to match on canvas the exact color and value of the object that you are trying to paint.

Most of the colors in nature are a combination of two or more of the colors on your palette and are slightly grayed up; in other words, not as brilliant as the raw color that comes straight out of the tube.

At first you may find it difficult to mix the grayed-up colors that you see before you. However, with practice you'll learn just which colors will produce the desired results.

All color can be roughly divided into warm or cool color. So when you look at a scene in nature, you must first decide whether the area that you wish to paint is on the warm or the cool side of your palette. When you have once decided on that point, you'll find it a lot easier to match the toned-down color that you see before you. For instance, most shadows are on the warm side, except when cooled off by the reflected blue of the sky. A shadow cast on a sandy beach from a boat pulled up on the shore would be cool where the blue sky could reflect down onto it, but would be warm under the boat where there would be no reflection from the sky. Shadows in rocks are quite warm except where a little of the cool color of the sky hits down on some of the top planes in shadow. Sunlight isn't quite as yellow or pink as you would expect it to be. When painting it, be sure that it has quite a lot of white in it and only a delicate amount of warmth. The only time that sunlight is really warm is just before the sunset when the sunlight has a strong orange-pink color. Sea water is a greenish blue close by, when you look directly into it; it becomes a more grayed-up blue in the distance where it picks up the color of the sky. When painting the foam of a cresting wave, the part in sunlight will be a little warm, while the shadows will be on the cool side.

PAINTING THE PICTURE

When you're ready to start the actual painting, begin first with the sky, as it sets the key for the whole picture. The sky color reflects down into all horizontal planes. If you have a stormy sky, your whole picture will have to be a stormy one, with the gray of the sky reflecting down onto all of the top planes of the picture. Sunny skies produce sunny pictures, with warm pinks and yellows throughout the picture. When starting the sky, you can paint rather thinly and without much finish, but at least cover the canvas with approximately the right color and value. Indicate any cloud formations at the same time. The sky in a marine should be toned down just a little, so that the white foam or the glitter on the water will be the lightest spot in the picture.

Next, start right in painting the water. Begin with your center of interest, which will probably be a cresting wave near the middle of your canvas. Paint

WRECKAGE *Sometimes the only clue to the fate of a missing boat will be some wreckage washed ashore after a storm. I used a simple color scheme in this picture: a warm gray sky, a little blue in the water, and brown in the rocks. I added a touch of orange to the oilskins of the middle figure and a little of the same color to some of the wreckage.*

THE ROCKBOUND COAST In this scene of a portion of the New England coast, the late afternoon light was from the right side of the picture. There were shadows over the foreground and on the left side of the rocks. This helped to give brilliance to the big cresting wave and the burst of spray in the background.

the foam of the breaking wave and the water around it. Also any adjacent rocks that are influencing the action of the wave.

As the depth of the water changes, you'll find that the spot where the waves crest will change also; so it's a good idea to get the wave action painted as quickly as possible. Decide just what you want the wave to be doing and stick to it. You can't change one part of the surf without changing the rest of it, as the action of each portion of the surf is influenced by, and is part of, the general movement of the whole mass of water. Never paint a wave as though it were all by itself in the picture. Always think of it in relation to the rest of the water.

Next lay in the rocks, but be careful to paint them in simple planes of light and shade in approximately two values.

I notice that in this chapter I am talking mostly about surf breaking on a rocky shore. Due to the varying depth of the water and the influence that the rocks have on the direction of the incoming waves, you'll find that the action of surf on a rocky shore is more complicated than on a sandy beach, where the breakers come straight into shore without being deflected by any rocks. However, you'll find that your picture of surf on a sandy beach has to be organized in the same manner and you paint it in the same order.

Starting with the important wave that will be your center of interest, you arrange the flattened-out waves moving in toward shore as decoratively as possible with the proper spacing between them. The trailing, floating foam from these waves will give interest and design to the foreground. Then the sand and any incidental details that you find, such as tide pools, driftwood, etc., can be indicated.

To summarize, when you start to paint, you will start with the sky. Next paint your important wave with the sea around it. Pattern off the flattened-out waves with their trailing foam. Then paint the beach and any details that will help give interest to the foreground.

9. Painting Surf on a Rocky Shore

You've probably noticed that I frequently repeat some of the same ideas in various chapters, although in slightly different language, for I believe that only by repetition can we get these points firmly fixed in our minds. I consider them so important that I'm running the risk of boring you by stating some of these principles over and over again.

Before starting to paint waves cresting on a rocky shore, you must know the direction in which they are moving, as well as their action.

Waves move in toward shore from the open sea in roughly parallel lines, and are evenly spaced. As they near the shore they head directly into each bay or inlet of the coastline, as shown in the accompanying diagram. When the waves reach the rocks, they surge over the smaller ones, but are deflected by the larger ledges and move around them, changing the direction of their forward movement and coming into shore at different angles.

A wave, while having mass and volume, is still fluid and pours around all solid objects in sweeping curves. This is why it's possible to give a fine, decorative design to the shapes of the breaking waves, and to the floating foam as it swirls around the rocks.

You have to paint the surf from memory, because it changes so fast it's almost impossible to get more than a fleeting glimpse of what the wave is doing. So, as I said above, if you know the direction in which the waves are moving and just what the action is, you'll find it easier to make a convincing statement of the scene before you.

STEP ONE

When you've decided just what you wish to paint, sketch in outline the shapes of all the important masses of light or dark in the picture. You will then know just exactly what your composition is going to look like.

After studying the surf for a few minutes, arrange the wave action in your sketch to correspond with the real movement of the sea. Plan the entire wave action at once and then stick to this design. Draw in the rocks and the kind of cloud formation that you see in the sky.

STEP TWO

Paint the sky in full value, using care not to make it too bright or important. Your real center of interest should be the water unless, as previously mentioned, you're painting a picture with the emphasis on the sky.

STEP THREE

Paint the breaking wave that is your center of interest, then the rest of the water around it. You can, at the start, suggest the modeling of the cresting wave by painting the shape of the shadows with a light blue-gray color and leaving the white canvas to suggest the light areas.

Be sure to space your waves correctly and remember that wherever you have a wave you'll have the trough alongside it.

STEP FOUR

Complete the rocks and the water next to them. Be sure that the rocks look as though they were really in the water and not just sitting on top of it. There will be reflections of the rocks in the clear water in front of them. Sometimes parts of the rocks underwater will be visible through the water if it isn't too deep.

Try to paint rocks in simple planes of light and shade in approximately two values. Wet rocks are darker than dry ones and have more of a glitter to them when the light is reflected from their wet surface. Rocks are mostly a warm gray color, though they vary in different localities. At least be careful not to make them too hot and eggy-looking in sunlight. It's a good idea to keep most shadows on rocks a little on the warm side unless they are cooled off by the cold light reflecting down onto them from the zenith of the sky. Leave the rocks looking a little unfinished. It's better to understate them. If you give them a high finish you can never get the water to look as convincing as the rocks, because the surf won't stand still to be painted.

Shadows in foam are generally a little cool if there's some warmth in the light areas of the foam.

SURF ON ROCKY SHORE Waves move in to shore in evenly spaced parallel lines. Closer to shore, the waves slightly change direction as they swing around the rocks and flow into each small opening I show in the diagram.

POINT LOBOS *I painted a number of pictures at Point Lobos on our last California trip. It was one of my favorite spots on the West Coast, with enough paintable material to keep me busy for weeks. No wonder some of the Western artists paint such fine seascapes!*

MT. DESERT ISLAND *This scene, created along the shore of Mt. Desert Island in Maine, was painted in a warm color scheme of browns, a warm gray and a dull gray-green.*

Finish up the picture. Paint in the light portions of the foam, add detail to cresting waves and floating foam. Also develop any secondary waves in the water. Repeat some of the sky color on the horizontal surfaces of the water. Next pull the sky together, softening edges where necessary.

Add accents either of color or of dark and light contrast to the foreground or your center of interest, and tone down any portion that conflicts with your center of interest.

Then take the picture home and try it in a frame. Generally a frame produces a minor miracle and often makes your picture look much better than you would have thought possible. Occasionally you're even startled to see how good it looks; at other times you're just merely startled.

However, don't be discouraged if your first few seascapes are a little less than the masterpieces you had hoped to paint. It requires a lot of practice and study of the sea to capture it on canvas. I doubt if even Winslow Homer was able to paint his great marine paintings without first messing up quite a lot of practice canvases.

STEP ONE The black-and-white pattern of the picture is blocked in.

STEP TWO The mood and color is set with the sky.

STEP THREE Major color areas are blocked in.

STEP FOUR Some refinements are made in the painting.

84

STRAITSMOUTH *Probably everyone who has ever visited Rockport, Massachusetts, remembers Straitsmouth Island and its light at the entrance of the harbor. This picture was painted one summer afternoon and shows the lighthouse and one end of The Island. The rocks on Cape Ann are a lovely shade of orangey pink, especially when seen in the late afternoon light. Collection, Dr. Clifford Hills.*

10. Painting Surf on a Sandy Beach

In the preceding chapter we were talking about painting surf on a rocky shore. This was really easy, because the rocky foreground was a great help in composing the picture. The rocks with their strong darks and decorative shapes gave you an interesting pattern of darks that contrasted pleasantly with the lighter masses of water and foam swirling around them.

UNDERSTANDING WATER ACTION

However, the action of the water itself is the most important thing in a marine painting. That's why surf coming in on a flat sandy beach can be just as thrilling as any other seascape. It just happens that most of my own painting has been done along the northern New England coast of the United States, which is predominantly rock bound. But I also enjoy painting in Florida, the Caribbean and Hawaii, where there are long stretches of sandy beaches.

Waves coming in on a sandy beach, because of the uniform depths of the water, generally crest for a much greater distance, and the wave appears much longer than on a rocky shore with its varying depths of water.

Due to the flatness of the beach, a wave after cresting will be carried by its own momentum a considerable distance up the beach. It gradually flattens

WAVES ON A SANDY BEACH *With no rocks to create varying depths of the water, waves crest for greater distances on a sandy beach.*

out and leaves a wake of foam trailing out behind it. When it reaches the end of its forward movement, it turns into floating foam which gradually disappears as the water flows out to sea again.

When the flattened-out wave gets into shallow water, it frequently changes its direction and continues inshore at a slightly different angle. This gives the effect of one wave, with its layer of water flowing over the wake of another wave at irregular intervals and at different levels. This produces a layer-like formation.

As long as a wave is still moving forward toward the beach, there is height and thickness in its front edge, while the trailing foam behind it is flatter and more lacy. The flattened-out curves of the front edges of these waves will help give interest and pattern to the foreground.

THE SANDY BEACH

The sand at the water's edge is darker when it's still wet from a preceding wave. This dark note will contrast with the light foam of the nearest wave, and will add weight and interest to the foreground.

Sometimes interesting lines are left on the sand from preceding waves. These lines are roughly parallel to the edge of the water, and are made by seaweed, driftwood, and other debris. Tidal pools in the sand or even small creeks trailing out toward the sea give variety and interest to the foreground.

As I've said earlier, you'll have more interesting lines in your picture if you look along the beach and paint the scene at an angle, rather than looking straight out to sea.

FOREGROUND WAVES

Because there isn't as much interesting detail on a sandy beach as there is on a rocky shore, you have to play up the design of your flattened foreground waves with their trailing pattern of floating foam. Look for a fine lacy pattern of the lighter foam against the darker color of the clear water. This will add foreground interest and will lead your eye into the picture.

The shallow water close to shore takes on the warm tone of the sand be-

WAVE FLATTENS OUT *The wave flattens out as it moves up the sandy shore, leaving a wake of foam trailing behind.*

SURF AT LONG BEACH   *In a sandy beach scene, the waves moving into shallow water can make a very decorative foreground. The slight change in direction of the waves as they go up the beach produces some interesting curves that lead the eye into the picture to the large cresting wave, the center of interest. Be sure that the waves in shallow water are painted in flat perspective so that they will appear to be on the same plane as the beach.*

FOREGROUND INTEREST   *The contours of the flattened-out edges in the waves give pattern and interest to the foreground. You can also include tide pools, logs, and seaweed to give added background interest.*

SURF AT CAPE MAY I painted this picture of the Jersey coast at an angle to take advantage of the interesting pattern of the flattened-out waves and tide pools in the foreground. It's difficult to suggest the size of these wonderful beaches. I remember getting a spectacular sunburn at Cape May one day when I was swimming instead of painting. I guess that there are always some days when we would all rather be beachcombers than artists.

89

neath it, and will be more of a tan color. Farther out, as the water gets deeper and you can't see much of the bottom, the water is more of a blue-green. The clear water of your cresting wave will be a rich, dark blue-green as you look straight into it and can see the color of the water itself.

PAINTING THE SKY

The sky is extremely important in a sandy beach picture, and should be made as interesting as possible. Whenever you have clouds in a sky, you can have cloud shadows over parts of your picture if you so desire. They are useful, because they enable you to concentrate the light exactly where you want it; also you can have dark shadowy spots anywhere they're needed, either on the land or on the water.

PAINTING THE PICTURE STEP-BY-STEP

The first step in painting surf on a sandy beach is to decide on the black-and-white pattern of the picture. Sketch in outline the shapes of all the masses of light and shade, from the sky down to the foreground. Next, paint in the sky, being careful to get the right value and color. After you've done this, paint in the big, cresting wave of your center of interest; also the flattened-out waves in the foreground. Try to get the shape of your floating foam at the same time, as well as the pattern of the surrounding water. Now paint the beach. Try to improve the pattern of your cresting waves and floating foam, as well as the distant sea. Then finish the picture. Add accents of color or tone to the center of interest and to the foreground. Pull the whole picture together by toning down unnecessary light spots and losing details wherever possible.

USING COLOR

A good picture should have a fine, decorative pattern of light and shade. Equally important is a harmonious and pleasing color scheme. I like a picture with comparatively few colors. I think it's generally stronger and more harmonious than one with a great many contrasting colors. That's why a picture with a back lighting that gives the effect of a warm glow over the whole picture is immensely effective. Some of the most striking pictures that I've done have been painted almost in black-and-white tones, with a single splash of brilliant color as an accent. Color is, after all, a very personal thing. No two people would see exactly the same colors in any given scene. I think if you just use good taste in your choice of color and avoid raw clashing colors, you should be able to paint some pleasing and harmonious pictures.

STEP ONE   *Sketch in the black-and-white pattern of your picture.*

STEP TWO   *Using the correct value and color, paint in the sky.*

91

STEP THREE   *Paint in the cresting wave and the foreground waves.*

STEP FOUR   *Paint in the beach and refine the details of the ocean.*

92

SANDY BEACH This picture was painted in Maine in the early fall. As a rule, marine paintings are inclined to be rather cool in color, but the brilliant sky in the York Beach scene gave a warm glow to the whole picture so that I was able to use warm color in the foreground surf and in the sandy beach. In the end, the entire picture was painted in an extremely warm color scheme.

THE HARBOR AT PORT CLYDE *This small land-locked harbor is the home port of the local lobstermen. I had been going to Port Clyde for years to get the boat for Monhegan Island, but I decided to paint some of the local scenery only recently. As you can see, it's a delightful spot and well worth painting.*

11. Open Sea Painting

An open sea painting without any foreground interest of rocks or sand has to have a careful arrangement of waves and foam in the foreground to lead your eye into the picture.

DESIGNING YOUR PICTURE

When painting the open sea, I think of the big swells as a series of mountain ranges with the smaller, secondary waves leading up to them like foothills in a landscape. Between each wave or mountain you have a corresponding trough or valley, so space your waves and be sure to get the proper contrast between the height of the waves and the trough between them.

A big wave cresting near the center of your picture would provide the usual center of interest. By working out a simple design for your masses of light foam and the large, dark shapes of the uncrested waves, you can work out a fine strong design of lights and darks. The sky becomes increasingly important and should have as much interest as possible.

WAVES IN OPEN SEA *Swells and waves can form an interesting arrangement in your painting.*

WINDY DAY   *Because I think that the sky is very important in an open sea picture, I decided to show a generous amount of it. I tried to design the pattern of the clouds to carry the interest from the upper right hand corner diagonally across the sky to the horizon on the left, then down the line of the cresting waves to the lower right hand corner, then back along the wave at the bottom of the picture. This makes use of the S-shaped composition that I use in a great many of my pictures.*

In most of the open sea pictures that I paint there's generally a boat, a raft, or some human interest. But if you do a good enough job painting the sky and sea, you won't have to depend on boats, seagulls, or people to add interest to your picture. To this end, I've known artists even to put mermaids or bathing beauties in their pictures. I think they're always fascinating to look at, but I suspect that a well-painted seascape will have a universal appeal without any added human interest.

LIGHT ON THE OPEN SEA

The lighting of an open seascape is extremely important and should be completely thought out in advance. A back lighting, you remember, is one in which you look into the light and all upright objects are silhouetted against the light beyond. In this way, you can have sharp, warm reflections of light on horizontal planes, while all the upright parts of waves and foam are in shadow. By having your strongest contrast of light and shade in the foreground and in your center of interest, you'll be able to concentrate the interest just where you need it.

*SOUTH SEAS   When you're painting a picture with cloud shadows on
the sea, you have complete freedom to use any design of light and shade
that you think will look right in the picture. In this painting, I silhouetted
the wave in the foreground against the lighter wave in the distance.*

When you look into the sun, the sky takes on a lot of warmth and you can
get a glow of warmth over the whole picture.

A diffused down light is another form of lighting that's effective, because
it enables you to paint everything in the picture in two planes, a light top plane
and a darker side plane. In this lighting, you get more of the local color of the
sky, sea, and waves than when painting with a back light. This is the effect
that you get on cloudy, foggy, or rainy days, as I mentioned earlier.

Another type of lighting—the side light—is most frequently used. It is always
effective, particularly when you combine it with a blue sky that has broken
clouds in it. This gives you the opportunity of using cloud shadows in your picture.

As previously mentioned, when you have cloud shadows on the sea, you have
a beautiful opportunity to use any portion of the picture as part either of your
light pattern or of the dark. A dark wave in the foreground silhouetted against
a lighter wave in full sunlight farther out in the picture is always effective.

STEP ONE   Draw in outline the shape of all the light and dark spots in the picture.

STEP TWO   Paint in the sky.

STEP THREE   Paint in the center of interest and suggestion of surrounding wave movement.

STEP FOUR   Lay in the remaining colors.

98

END OF THE DAY   *Some years ago when we were on a freighter trip to Puerto Rico, I was impressed by the rather ominous look of the sea in the late afternoon sunlight. It looked to me as though we might have some nasty weather coming up. However, not a thing happened and when we arrived in San Juan the next day. The weather was lovely. I painted the picture later in my studio from a sketch I had made on the ship.*

A FISHING PORT There's always life and activity around a harbor, but it seldom disturbs the general mood of peace and tranquility. This is a light picture with balanced dark spots.

First decide on the black-and-white pattern of your picture; outline the shapes of all the masses of light and dark in your picture. An open sea picture is generally painted in the studio from memory, or from quick sketches made at sea. You can, therefore, use any color scheme and light effect that appeals to you. As previously noted, you have to arrange the foreground waves in an effective and decorative pattern of light and shade in order to lend interest to the foreground and to lead your eye back into the picture to your center of interest.

After you've done this, paint the sky in the usual way.

Next, paint the cresting wave that is your center of interest; then the foreground waves that lead the eye into the picture and the water around them.

Then paint the distant ocean, taking care to see that the color of the sky is reflected in the distant sea. Add detail to the cresting wave that is the center of interest, and further develop the foreground waves.

Now complete the picture in the usual way. It's a good idea, when finishing the picture, to stop before it's entirely done. We all have a tendency to overwork a picture. All the thousand and one fancy touches that we add at the last minute seldom improve the picture. There's an old saying, that it takes two people to paint a masterpiece: one to do the painting, the other one to hit him over the head with a hammer at the proper moment before the artist has a chance to spoil the picture. I'll bet that our wives (or husbands) would be only too willing to do a little work with the hammer when they see a fine vigorous sketch being ruined by too many finishing touches.

12. Drawing Boats

The average landsman doesn't know very much about boats, although I doubt if he's in the class of a former Secretary of the Navy. This great man was reported to have said the first time he saw a submarine surface and some of the crew come out of the conning tower, "Gosh, the darned thing's hollow."

Well, let's start from there. Yes, boats are hollow and float *on* and *in* the water. The simplest way to think of a boat is that it's a long, narrow box with one end pointed. Probably the first boats were just hollowed-out logs with pointed ends or crude rafts without any pleasing lines at all.

Although occasionally you see someone paint a harbor scene in which the boats bear a strong resemblance to canoes, gondolas, or the type of craft used by Columbus when he discovered America, fortunately it's not necessary to go back to the early days to find interesting ships to paint. Our present-day boats are picturesque and fascinating enough to suit anyone so we'll just concentrate on them.

Boats can be divided roughly into two categories—small boats that operate off a beach or in harbors, and the larger, seagoing ships that are at home in deep water.

SIMPLE NAUTICAL TERMS

Before going any further, I'd like to mention some of the simpler nautical terms with which we should all be familiar when describing boats.

The front end of a boat is called the *bow*; the rear portion, the *stern*. When we speak of going or looking toward the rear of a ship, we say "going aft" or "looking aft" or the "after" part of the ship, and when going toward the front, we speak of the "fore" part of the boat or "going forward." The expressions *fore* and *aft* mean bow and stern.

The width from side to side is called the *beam*.

The floor is always called the *deck*. The sides of an open boat are called the *gunwales*.

The right side of a boat looking forward is called the *starboard side* and the left, the *port side*. The rudder and steering gear are called the *helm*. The man who steers is the *helmsman*.

CONSTRUCTION OF THE BOAT

It isn't necessary to know all the technical details about boat building in order to paint boats convincingly, so without getting too involved in marine construc-

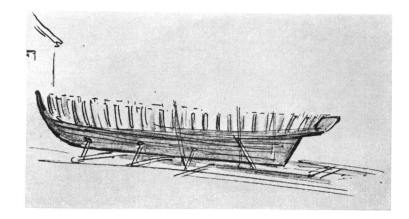

CONSTRUCTION OF BOAT *Just as ribs and backbone form the central support in the human body, so do the keel and timbers support the boat.*

tion I'll try to explain in the simplest possible manner the important characteristics that you'll have to remember when drawing a boat.

You have to be familiar, first, with the shape of the boat; next, the way she sits in the water and, then, the general purpose of her fittings and equipment.

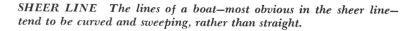

SHEER LINE *The lines of a boat—most obvious in the sheer line— tend to be curved and sweeping, rather than straight.*

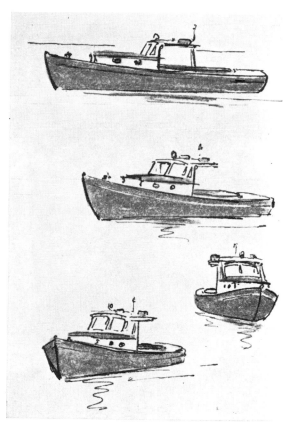

103

SHEER LINE   It helps to see the curves of the boat by reducing the sheer line to a simple figure eight formation.

The frame of a ship looks a little like a human skeleton, the keel and timbers resemble the ribs and backbone of a person. At one end of the keel is the stem, at the other, the stern post. The closely spaced rib timbers are in between.

SHEER LINE

Every part of a boat is designed either for utility, added strength, or seaworthiness. The bow of a boat stands higher out of the water than the stern in order to ride the waves better.

The line of the deck or *sheer line* has a pleasant dip from bow to stern which must be thoroughly understood and carefully drawn, because it determines the appearance of the whole vessel. The lines of a boat are usually long, sweeping curves rather than straight lines. I think this is one reason the inexperienced

STEM   The structure of the stem is clearly visible.

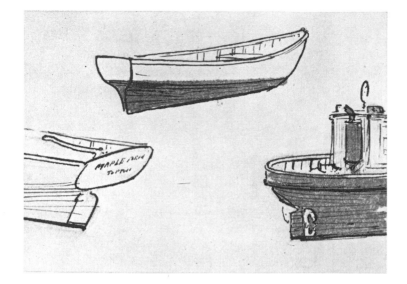

STERN   *Sterns are generally squared-off or rounded.*

marine painter has so much trouble with boats—he tries to draw them with straight lines, the way he would draw a house, rather than with curved lines.

It may help, when drawing the sheer line of a boat, to think of a figure eight. Sometimes the figure isn't easy to see, but it exists in rhythm just the same.

STEM AND STERN

The stem of a boat, that is, the piece of timber running up the bow of the boat, is clearly visible from the outside. While some small boats—like lifeboats and seine boats—are double-ended with the rudder attached to the after end, most boats have squared-off or rounded sterns.

One familiar type of stern looks as though the rear of the boat had been sawed off at a slightly sloping angle. This is called a *transom stern*. From the rear it looks a little like a wineglass.

Another variation is the counter-stern, which continues out for some distance past the rudder and overhangs the water. This is a particularly graceful style of stern and is often seen in racing yachts in an exaggerated form. Another type gives the ship a rounded end which overhangs the stern post and provides a maximum amount of deck space.

PLANKING AND MOLDING

There are two chief methods of planking a wooden vessel, the *carvel* and the *clincker-built*. In the carvel the planks are laid edge to edge, which gives a smooth-sided effect, while with the clincker-built the planks overlap. This latter system is seen in dinghies, rowboats, and small coastal fishing boats.

On the outside of the hull, at the deck level, you'll notice a heavy piece of molding. This is called the *fender rail* or *rubbing strake* and protects the hull from rubbing and from the minor impacts that all boats must sustain. Often this molding is covered with a flat strip of iron to give greater durability and added protection.

105

All boats, with the exception of barges or flat-bottomed rowboats, have a keel which is an integral part of the boat. In sailing boats, the keel prevents the boat from sliding bodily sidewise to leeward. In all types of vessels the keel, of varying depths, adds to the maneuverability of the boat and makes it steadier and safer at sea.

RELATING HORIZON LINE TO BOAT

When drawing a boat, you have to keep in mind where your eye line or the horizon line is, and then you must study the sheer of the boat. Usually, owing to the high bow and the comparatively low stern, the top lines of the hull instead of going up to the horizon line as they recede, often slant the opposite way, going down as they recede. As it recedes, the water line of the vessel, however, goes up to meet the horizon line in the expected direction.

When drawing a boat that's a little foreshortened—one that's pointed slightly toward or away from you—be careful not to have the water line of the ship point down too sharply as it approaches you, because this is liable to make the water tilt down and not lie flat on the water plane. It's only when you're looking down on a boat quite nearby that you have very exaggerated perspective. Farther off, near the horizon, all lines are practically horizontal anyway with very little drop to them as they approach.

KEEL Vital to the stability and maneuverability of the boat, the keel varies in shape according to the vessel.

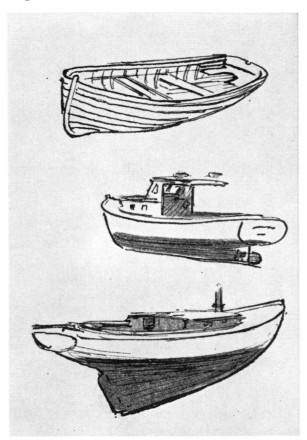

SUPERSTRUCTURE *The position of the superstructure also varies according to the size and function of the vessel.*

Be sure to remember where your eye or horizon line is when drawing boats that are different distances away in a harbor. If, for instance, your eye line is that of a man standing on the deck of a ship, the eyes of all other men standing on a deck of the same height would be on the same level no matter where they were in the harbor. Everything below your eye level would go up to the horizon line as it receded and everything above would go down to it. For instance, the top of a pilothouse, being above your eye line, would slant down toward the horizon; halfway across the harbor it would be nearer the horizon line, hence more nearly horizontal, but still above it.

When painting boats in the comparatively still water of a harbor, always consider the reflections of the vessel in the water as an integral part of the boat and draw in the reflections at the same time that you're drawing the boat. We'll discuss the painting of reflections at greater length in the next chapter.

SMALL BOATS

Small boats also have fascinating lines, but a flat-bottomed skiff hasn't quite as graceful a sheer as a dinghy or an ordinary rowboat. A popular type of rowboat, the dory, is also flat-bottomed with a very narrow stern which makes it look almost double-ended. It is sturdily built, will stand rough usage, and is a fine seaboat.

107

SAILBOATS

Sailboats are the most decorative kind of boats and it's a shame that, except for pleasure yachts, they're rarely seen any more. I wish that this book could have been written fifty or sixty years ago when there were still sailing vessels along the coasts. There are still a few small sloops and schooners in the Caribbean and other less civilized spots and we shall talk about them in a later chapter.

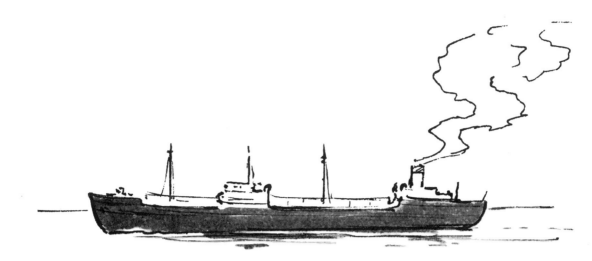

SUPERSTRUCTURE *Notice that the superstructure on an oil tanker is spread out from fore to aft.*

MASTS AND SUPERSTRUCTURE

The masts and superstructure of a boat are important since they add greatly to the decorative appearance of the ship. In sailing vessels, masts are still used for their original purposes to support the sails, but in all other types of vessels that do not depend on sails for locomotion, the masts are used mainly as hoists for handling cargo or for displaying flags, lights or signals.

The superstructure always includes a wheelhouse or pilothouse, cabins for officers or crew, and space for portions of the engine or motor. Sometimes this deckhouse is amidships and sometimes aft, depending on the type of vessel. Most small or medium-sized trawlers or draggers have the pilothouse and the rest of the housing at the stern to allow more room for handling cargo. Tugs have the deckhouse a little forward of amidships, while most freighters have the bridge, pilothouse, and cabins amidships. Oil tankers sometimes have the bridge, pilothouse, and cabins amidships and the smokestack, deckhouse, and lifeboats at the stern. Most passenger liners and passenger-carrying freighters have the superstructure amidships.

EQUIPMENT ON THE BOAT

It helps in drawing a ship if you know what the more important pieces of equipment are used for—so let's consider a small dragger, and I will explain the function of the different objects that you see cluttering up the decks. From bow to stern we see (1) *hawsehole,* (2) metal posts for making lines fast called *bitts,* (3) *anchor,* (4) *forward hatch* leading to the cabin below, (5) tin stovepipe of the cooking stove, called the *galley stack,* (6) *ventilator,* (7) *hoists* or *galluses* used in seining. They carry the strain of the nets and the wooden boards called (8) *doors* that keep the mouth of the nets or "drags" open, (9) *mast with boom,* (10) rope ladders, (11) ropes that support the masts called *standing rigging* and lines for handling gear called *running rigging.* (12) *masthead light,* (13) nets drying in the sun, (14) *windlass* or *winch* used for handling nets or unloading cargo, (15) pilothouse with (16) running lights and wooden shields, (17) radio compass and antenna, also (18) radar equipment and (19) spotlights on the roof, (20) muffler and exhaust pipe for motor, (21) *dory* on wooden supports at the stern. Below each hoist up forward is an iron sheathing (22) that protects the hull from damage when hoisting the heavy doors aboard ship. This sheathing generally loes its paint and gets rusty, forming a nice orange-red spot of color to break up the ship's side. Nowadays, as a rule, the dory and masts are painted a bright orangy yellow for better visibility at sea. The *fender rail* (23) is at deck level; above it are the *scuppers*, which are openings to allow water to drain off the decks.

EQUIPMENT *Each item indicated on this small dragger serves a function, which is described in the text. Understanding their functions will help you to paint these details more convincingly.*

ST. CROIX *This scene is part of the harbor at Christiansted, painted from the Club Comanche.*

GLOUCESTER DRAGGER   *In this early morning scene, you could see almost perfect reflections of the boats in the quiet waters of the harbor.*

13. Harbors

Now that we've learned something about boats, let's proceed to study the harbor scenes.

REFLECTIONS

When painting the more or less still water of a harbor, it helps to think of the water as a large, flat mirror in which everything above is reflected in the water below. Because the water usually presents a level surface to the sky, it will take on the modified color of the sky except close at hand, where you look right down into the water and see the greenish color of the water itself or of the muddy or sandy bottom.

If you keep in mind a few simple facts about reflections, I'm sure that you won't have too much trouble painting them. Remember that the reflection of every point is located underneath it as far below the water line as the point is above it.

Because water is not a perfect reflecting surface, light objects will reflect a little darker than they are; reflections of medium-toned objects, being neither light nor dark, will reflect exactly the same value as the object itself; dark values will sometimes reflect a little lighter than they really are. If your eye line is near the surface of the water, any object will reflect a perfect inverted image of itself in the water. Since your eye line usually is considerably above the surface of the water, the reflections of objects never look the way they do in direct sight.

When you look at any object and its reflection in the water, the object is seen

ANGLE OF REFLECTION   *The angle of incidence is equal to the angle of reflection.*

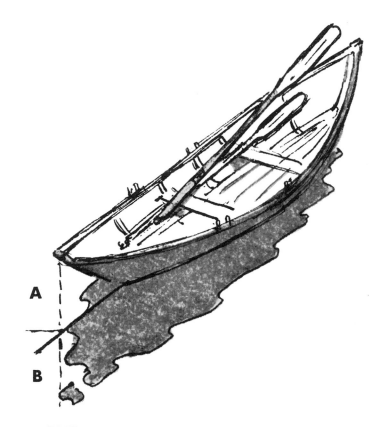

REFLECTIONS *Note the difference between the way the boat appears in direct vision from the way it appears in the reflection.*

directly by the eye, while the reflection is viewed in an indirect line that runs down to the surface of the water about midway between you and the object, then continues upward from the surface of the water to the object reflected. In the line of reflected sight the angle of incidence from the object to the water is equal to the angle of reflection from the object to the observer. Things that are in sight by direct vision are often not reflected in the water and, inversely, the underside of a wharf will be seen in the reflection. You appear to be looking up at an otherwise invisible object. The sketch of the dory shows the difference between the way the boat looks in direct vision and the way it's reflected in the water.

To determine the length of a reflection, remember the previously stated rule: "the reflection of an object is located directly underneath and as far below the reflecting surface as the object is above it." For example, a single pile set vertically in the water has a perfect inverted image. But, when a pile leans toward you, its length above the water is slightly foreshortened. The length of the reflection, therefore, is longer than the apparent length of the pile. You will find the proper length of this reflection by observing the distance from the top of the pile to the water directly beneath it, and, following our rule, the near end of this reflection is the same distance below the reflecting surface as the top of the pile is above it. In the case of a pile that is tilted away from you, its reflection is shorter than the pile itself. You will see the application of our rule about reflections as you study the sketch of the piles.

113

When painting the still surface of a harbor, you'll notice that the water near you appears darker when you look down into it because there's less reflected light from the sky to brighten it. A little farther from you, the water is lighter with an occasional brilliant reflection on some of the ripples. Still farther from you, the water may look slightly darker with alternating strips of lighter and darker tones. These are caused by areas of smooth water in contrast to the rough areas that are ruffled by the wind. The smooth water reflects only the sky, while the rougher water reflects light from many directions. If the light source originates in the background of the picture, the rough water will pick up a brilliant glitter from the sun and will be lighter than the smoother portions that reflect the sky. Sometimes the rougher portions may be darker, according to the prevailing light effects. In any case, you can paint these areas like long, narrow, horizontal wedges, being careful to keep them narrower and closer together as they recede toward the horizon.

Even the comparatively still water of the bay is never completely still. There will always be small ripples coming in toward shore in parallel lines from the direction the wind is blowing or from the more open parts of the harbor. It's important to note the direction of these small ripples because they give a wavy, wiggly shape to the edges of your reflections and add greatly to the charm of the scene. If these little waves are large enough, they will break up the reflections with some crisp, light, possibly horizontal touches that make an effective contrast to the vertical lines of the reflections. It's always a good plan to paint the reflections up and down, using vertical brush strokes, and to paint the ripples with horizontal strokes.

LENGTH OF REFLECTION *Note the relationship between the actual pile (A) above the surface of the water (B) and the reflection (C) below the surface.*

FIGURES *An effective way to paint figures is to silhouette them against a light background.*

WHARFS

Wharfs are fun to paint because they have dark shadows under them, and the piles covered with scum and seaweed are quite decorative. The planking of a wharf is laid on crossbeams that are bolted onto the supporting piles. Around the outside of the wharf you'll notice a row of piles that are a protection for the wharf itself; they also cushion the shock when some mariner docks his ship with too much energy.

The cluster of piles at the corners of a wharf are for added strength. The taller piles are for mooring boats while the short ones are to protect the wharf. The old stone piers have piles along the edge to protect the ships that are tied alongside. The occasional wooden ladders reaching down the side of the wharf to the water add interest to the scene.

SHACKS

The shacks and warehouses seen on the wharfs are often decrepit and very picturesque in appearance. Unfortunately the newer buildings are so clean and neat that they aren't too interesting to paint. Generally, I try to make the buildings on a wharf look as weathered as possible. Such a practice worries the proud owner of the property, who does not like to see his tidy new building suddenly look so old, but it does add to the fun of the painting and gives the picture much more charm and atmosphere.

HUMAN FIGURES

Figures add greatly to the picture's interest. Perhaps it's the human element that attracts one's attention, but I do know that the eye is immediately attracted by figures in a picture. They're the first things noticed and are always the center of interest. When you're painting a harbor scene, however, your chief interest should be a particular boat or a cluster of boats and perhaps some portion of waterside scenery, so you must be very careful where figures are placed. Preferably they should be placed near the center of interest, or where they will focus attention upon those parts of your picture which you wish to accent.

First, be sure that the figure is the right size, that is, in scale with its surroundings. Then, draw the figure in the pose and action that you think will go well with the rest of the picture. Paint the figure as a simple spot or silhouette. Don't overmodel it or add too many details. It's surprising how convincing a small figure looks when handled in this simple manner. The head and arms might be a medium dark spot, the shirt a flat dark note—perhaps red—and the trousers a lighter shade. Most of the time figures can be painted as slightly dark silhouettes. Only if they're in strong light against a dark background should they be lighter spots in a picture.

SEA GULLS

Another way to add life and movement to a picture is to put in some sea gulls. They can be very effective and decorative if they're used in the right spots. Unfortunately, most of the gulls that you see in pictures seem to be all out of shape and resemble neither fish nor fowl. They sometimes look like fat, decrepit pigeons or mosquitoes that couldn't stay in the air for a second unless someone held them there.

A sea gull is a stupid bird without a trace of individuality. All he can do is to fly and swim a little. However, he flies and soars superbly and is very decorative. It will help if you remember that sea gulls are mostly wings, their bodies small and streamlined—never fat. The herring gull, most common along the New England coast, is brown and tan when young, but white and gray when grown, with black wing-tips.

When painting a number of gulls, slant them at different angles, and by having a number of their silhouettes overlap a decorative pattern can be arranged which will make an interesting design in your picture.

HARBOR SCENERY

It also adds interest to your picture to put in some of the picturesque junk that you see on some of the older wharfs—such objects as crates, oil drums and assorted barrels, lobster pots, hoists for unloading cargoes, old tarpaulins, ropes, and nets.

I personally like to paint shipyards with a boat up on the ways, or rowboats pulled up on a shelving beach, showing also the small shacks nearby for storage of fishermen's gear.

116

There is something about looking at a peaceful harbor that is infinitely soothing and comforting to me. I think that it's good for one's soul. A painting of it often has the same restful effect. Perhaps this is the reason that harbor scenes are universally popular.

MOONLIT HARBOR   *This picture of the deserted waterfront was painted at Glouces-*
ter, Massachusetts. I drew in the scene on a 20 x 30 canvas on the spot. That evening,
I came back and studied the scene from the same location. Then I painted the picture in
the studio the next day.

HOME FROM THE SEA   *The dragger in this picture had discharged its cargo of fish and was going over to its own particular wharf to be tied up for the weekend. In a harbor scene, I like to occasionally paint a ship under way, instead of always painting the ship tied up to a dock.*

14. Planning a Harbor Painting

Before I start out for a day's painting, I carefully check my equipment to be sure that I haven't forgotten something of vital importance such as zinc white or my easel. It's horrible to discover, when you're ready to paint, that something is missing. Once I got all the way to the Virgin Islands before I discovered that I had left my brushes behind!

When you get to the waterfront, look the scene over carefully and select a view that interests you. If it appeals to you and looks as though it would make a good picture, paint it. Don't waste time trying to find something better because you may not find it.

It's better to avoid a complicated subject such as the panorama of an entire harbor. Choose a simpler subject—just a boat and part of a wharf or some old tumbled-down fishhouses. Next, look at the scene from several different directions to be sure that you have the angle that will give the most pleasing arrangement of the areas of light and shade. Then note the direction of the light and of the sun. You can thus anticipate the changing light and later you won't have to make any drastic changes in your pattern of light and shade. It also helps to have a schedule of the tides so that you can tell whether they're rising or falling and can accordingly make your plans.

Don't let the fact that a scene has already been painted by other artists bother you. Practically everything interesting has been painted many times but probably not the way *you* will paint it. Often a commonplace subject can be made immensely interesting by the way you place it on your canvas or by painting it from a slightly different angle. After all, the same scene looks a little different to everyone because no two individuals see alike, and your picture should reflect this difference.

When you've decided on your subject matter, the angle from which you wish to paint it, and the anticipated changes in light and shade, you might then study it through your view finder to decide just what portion of the scene to include in your picture. There's so much to see outdoors anyway, it's always necessary to eliminate the unimportant and concentrate on the important elements of your scene.

PRELIMINARY SKETCHES

Before starting to draw in your picture, it always helps to make one or two small pencil sketches of the scene to be sure that you have a good dark and light

119

SKETCH When you have an idea of what you want to paint, draw one or two sketches to plot out the black-and-white pattern.

FINISHED PAINTING Notice that the over-all pattern of the painting is very much the same as the pattern established in the sketch.

121

ROCKPORT *I tried to maintain a strong foreground interest, contrasted with a rather hazy effect in the background.*

design for your painting. Remember that you have only one real center of interest in your picture. It can be a group of boats tied up at a wharf or a mass of old buildings, but it must dominate the scene and first attract the eye. Everything else in the picture must be subordinated to it or lead the eye toward that center of interest.

Every artist should always carry a small drawing pad and form the habit of making quick sketches of interesting scenes. These sketches are of the greatest value when painting away from the shore. You'll find that you can remember things much better if you take time to make a sketch of them. Even a hasty sketch will help you recall a scene more vividly.

I have occasionally tried taking a photograph of something that interested me instead of sketching it. This seems to work out very well for a great many artists, but not for me. When I look at the photograph I have taken of a scene, I can't figure out what the different blobs of light and shade are supposed to be. The fact that I am the world's worst photographer may have something to do with this lack of success. I do know that many artists, particularly illustrators, depend on photography to a great extent and seem to have very successful results.

When you've decided on the scene you want to paint, you'll sometimes find it makes a perfect composition. In that case, you're in luck and will have nothing to worry about except painting what you see in front of you. Occasionally, however, you'll find the composition is not ideal, and you'll have to eliminate a few objectionable objects or move things around a little to make a more decorative composition. This is perfectly all right. Since an artist isn't a camera he should use his own judgment and good taste in deciding what to include and what to eliminate in his picture.

PAINTING IN COMFORT

When painting outdoors, be sure to have your canvas in shadow, because it's impossible to see color correctly if the sun is shining directly on your picture. You'll discover that direct sunlight gives a nice, warm glow over everything, and a sketch that looks warm and brilliant in the sun will look cold and gray when you look at it back in the studio. Bright sunlight on a canvas is rather blinding to look at and certainly doesn't help your eyes. I generally carry two canvases of the same size and put one in back of the other on my easel so that the sun doesn't shine through the canvas on which I'm working. Since I usually work on one canvas in the morning and the other one in the afternoon, it's very convenient to have them both right at hand when I need them.

After you've selected your subjects and are ready to start the picture, be sure that you're in a comfortable spot for working. If you stand, have something smooth to stand on; if you like to paint sitting down, be sure that you have a good place for your stool and easel. Nothing can be more disconcerting than to step back into a crevice in the rocks or have the rotten planking of a wharf give way unexpectedly and deposit you in the water. Besides, if you're uncomfortable when you're painting, it may show in your picture. It's difficult to create an effect of carefree abandon in your painting if you're balanced uncomfortably on one foot or teetering on a stool that feels as though it were ready to capsize at any moment.

STEP ONE *When you start a picture, first draw in outline all the objects that appear in the painting. Then paint in the sky and its reflections in the distant water.*

THE GREEN BOAT *Tone down the value of the wharf and add any necessary accents and details to the rest of the picture.*

15. Painting a Harbor Scene

When you've made up your mind what you're going to paint in the harbor scene, wade right into it and paint it while you're still full of enthusiasm for your subject. A picture that's of interest to the artist is generally of interest to everyone else.

It's also a fine thing to finish the picture, if possible, while you're still excited about it, because it usually has a dash and brilliance that's hard to achieve in a worked-over job. I find that when I spend too much time on a picture I lose interest in it and the thing begins to fall apart.

EARLY STAGES

Generally I try to lay in most of the picture at one sitting, so that I have only details to finish up later. This means trying to hit the exact color and value of each part of my painting as I go along. First, I figure out the arrangement of all the objects that are to go in the painting, taking care to arrange them as decoratively as possible. Next, I draw in the outline of all the big masses of light and shade in the picture. Then I start painting the sky and its reflections in the water, because the sky sets the key for the whole painting.

Now lay in the dark masses, starting at the center of interest. Try to get the right values and color as you go along. Next put in the medium tones, comparing them to the lightest lights and darkest darks. Be sure to keep the dark pattern simple and don't break it up with too many lights. The same thing applies to the lights—be careful not to get the halftones in the lights too dark, because they will break up the light pattern and spoil the design of the whole picture.

PUTTING IN THE COLOR

Now consider the color. While the values in your picture are perhaps more important to consider at the start because they're the framework upon which you construct the whole painting, you must, nevertheless, have a fine, harmonious color scheme as well. Some beginners try to fill their pictures with every kind of color in the world—all of it nice and bright and right out of the tube. In fact, the greater variety of colors they can get into a sketch, the happier they seem to be. But it's safer to use only a few colors, as I've said earlier. The picture will look less confusing and have more harmony.

Always try to consider color in a picture as being either on the warm side or the cool, just as you did when you painted the surf. The most effective pictures are either predominantly warm with a few cool accents or else cool with warm spots. Don't have too equal a division of warm and cool color in a picture because the effect isn't as striking as when one or the other predominates. Most of the color in a picture is a little grayed up, and strong color is only used in a few accents, mostly in the foreground.

After studying the color in the scene you're to paint, try to decide whether the important colors in the scene are warm or cool. If it's hard to decide whether an area is on the warm side or the cool, compare it to the more brilliant colors in the picture that are definitely warm or cool. In this way, you can usually decide which way to slant the color.

Your strongest color should be in your center of interest and in the foreground. If you're doing a sunlight scene, you'll find a lot of warm color reflected from your sunlit areas into the adjacent shadows. In fact, you can use warmer colors in these spots than in the light areas. In painting sunlight, you have to be careful not to get it too warm. It's only the late afternoon sun that has the pinky orange glow to it. If you paint midday sun with that much warmth in it, you will find that it has an eggy look.

Generally, keep as much warmth as possible in your shadows; this will give them depth. Any horizontal surfaces in the shadow that are open to the sky will pick up some of the cool color from the sky. For instance, the shadow of a dory on a sandy beach will be cool wherever the sky can reflect down into the shadow, but under the side of the dory, where the light from the sky can't penetrate, the shadow will be quite warm.

Working outdoors in the full light of day you can slightly intensify the color in your picture since it will look a little cooler and grayer in the half-light indoors.

Remember to keep your color clean and fresh-looking by mixing only a little of it on your palette and by applying the paint directly to the different areas of the painting—then not working over it any more than necessary.

DIRECT PAINTING

Direct painting requires good draftsmanship. You can't slop around any old way and hope for the best. You have to know exactly what you want to do and do it without any waste of time.

You can't paint faster than you can think. This means that you have to decide in your mind what you want to do before you do it. Your thinking has to keep ahead of your brushwork.

While some very fine pictures have been made by underpainting and glazing, that type of painting is more for studio work. Certainly, direct painting is the only practical method for outdoor work.

CHRISTIANSTED HARBOR *St. Croix in the Virgin Islands is one of our favorite spots. We spent many happy holidays there at the hotel which is located on a small island in the harbor at Christiansted. The only contact with the shore was by boat. A husky man ferried supplies, baggage, and guests back and forth all day long. The boats in the distance probably came over from Trinidad with a variety of interesting cargoes. In the Caribbean, the water is often the almost unbelievable shade of blue that you see in this picture.*

NORTHEASTER On Cape Ann, there are frequent periods when there's very little surf to paint. However, when the wind gets around to the Northeast, there's as much surf as anyone could desire. If you want the wave to look large and impressive, try to paint the scene from as low a viewpoint as possible.

16. Sea and Harbor by Day and Night

I think that if you want to do a great many pictures of the sea, or of harbors, it's fun to paint them in various moods and with different light effects. This will help you get away from the usual marine with its nice blue sky, green sea, and brownish rocks, or a harbor scene with its green water, white boats and brown shacks and wharfs.

MOONLIGHT SCENES

One of the most fascinating effects in nature is moonlight. It's lovely anywhere, but over the sea it's particularly striking and is well worth trying to paint.

Moonlight scenes are always mysterious and beautiful, particularly in surf or harbor scenes. It's possible to suggest so much with so little detail. Unfortunately, moonlight scenes have to be done from memory, but I think that if you start your picture as soon as possible after viewing the moonlit harbor, you'll still have a pretty good mental impression of the scene the next day.

Moonlight is cooler and much weaker than sunlight; as a result, the shadows are darker and simpler. Light spots have little detail in them and shadows practically none. You can see the big division of light and shade, but that's about all.

While moonlight is cooler than sunlight, I try to avoid painting everything blue or green, because there's warmth in the shadows as well as throughout the entire picture. You can keep quite a little warmth in the darks and a little in the moonlight itself. Many artists seem to think that a moonlight scene is simply a daytime picture painted blue. This is far from the case, as you will observe when you study moonlight and see how it really looks.

I generally paint the sea, sky, foam, and rocks in varying shades of warm blue-green that sometimes verge on purple. The strong darks in the foreground should be warmer than those farther back in the picture. And often I paint a moonlight marine with a back light hitting on the sea and silhouetting waves and rocks against the light. If you don't show the moon itself, you can suggest its location just above the top of the picture either by showing its light on clouds near the top of the picture or by painting a blur of light in the sky itself, extending down into the picture. When you don't show the source of light, you can go as high in key as you wish on the light hitting into your picture.

With the exception of the brilliant path of moonlight down through the middle of your picture, most edges will be soft or entirely lost. It will be difficult to see

TWILIGHT *This West Coast scene was painted in my studio from a sketch that I made on the spot. The sky was a strong orangey yellow while the foreground was mostly in shadow. The rocks were a brownish purple with a little cool blue green on their top planes. The surf in shadow was a pale blue-green. Twilight scenes, such as this, give an effect of little detail and color, but strong simple patterns of light and shade.*

the horizon line except in the path of moonlight, and even the edges of the light foam in shadow will be soft and almost lost.

All the lost edges add greatly to the effect of mystery which is part of the charm of a moonlight scene.

An effective way to paint a moonlit harbor is to use a back lighting with the moonlight reflecting on the water and boats or on the shacks silhouetted against the light.

On the other hand, when you do show the moon itself, the rest of the lights have to be toned down to make the moon look sufficiently bright, so that you have very little sparkle left for the rest of the picture. The only time that you can safely show the moon is when there is still some light from the setting sun to provide the general lighting for the entire picture. In this case, the moon won't be bright enough to be the source of light. This kind of picture can be breathtakingly beautiful if it's well done. It is, however, really more of a sunset than a moonlight effect.

THE MOONLIT SEA   The only trouble with a moonlight seascape is that when you find nice moonlight, there's generally very little surf. However, once in a while you're lucky. I painted this picture in my studio at Pigeon Cove after studying the moonlight and surf over at Bass Rocks the night before.

SUNSET SCENES

While sunset and twilight scenes are sometimes considered too sweet and sentimental to paint, I like them and I think almost everyone else does too. There isn't anything wrong with this type of picture. It's just the cheap and gaudy way they've been painted by so many buckeye artists over the years that has rather dimmed their popularity in the upper art circles.

In a sunset picture, the sky is the real center of interest and the sea or harbor is only important in that it reflects some of the brilliance of the sky.

A sunset has to be done chiefly from memory since it changes every minute and hardly ever lasts long enough for you to make more than a few hasty notes of the color and shape of the more important clouds. To see the most brilliant color, you usually look into a sunset. Therefore, you'll have a scene with a back lighting, with the sky and its reflections in the water forming your light pattern and everything else forming part of your dark pattern. It's better not to show the sun itself but to have it behind a cloud or just below the horizon with its brilliant lights reflected on the clouds and the still water of the harbor. You will thus find

135

that a lot of the warmth of the sky will be reflected down into the whole foreground, particularly on the horizontal planes.

Your painting of a sunset can never be as brilliant as the real sunset because you can only approximate the value of light itself with the limited range of oil paints. You'll find that it's difficult to get sufficient strength of color into the sky and at the same time to get the sky light enough. To do this, you'll have to use a good deal of white with your color, particularly with the reds, which are rather low-keyed colors. It's probably just as well that we can't reproduce all this brilliance on our canvas, since nature produces some rip-roaring effects that, in a picture, would look like the gaudiest kind of calendar art.

TWILIGHT SCENES

There's a lovely tranquil feeling about a twilight scene that has a great appeal for me. I like the simple pattern of light and shade that you see before dark. The sky and its reflections in the water are the light pattern, and everything else is part of a darker silhouette. The whole picture could be painted almost entirely in two tones of light and shade with very few colors and only a little detail in the center of interest or in the foreground.

The more colors you use, the more complicated your picture becomes. Some of the strongest and most effective pictures are those painted with an analogous color scheme; that is, just a few related warm colors or a cool scheme with cool colors. In either, a single touch of a complementary color will make an effective accent.

I'll sometimes paint an entire picture in tones of warm pink or tan with just a touch of cool green or blue as an accent. The result looks surprisingly convincing and gives the effect of full color.

It's fun to go out at sunset to some favorite spot along the waterfront and study the scene before you as it changes from twilight to dusk. If the light permits, make a simple pencil sketch of the pattern of light and shade, jotting down the general color of the large areas in the picture. In your studio the next day, try painting the scene as you remember it with the aid of your sketch and penciled notes. You can often produce an extremely convincing picture with the real spirit of twilight in it.

FOG AND RAIN SCENES

The sea or harbor is fascinating in fog or rain and certainly interesting to paint under these conditions. A fog scene has mystery and can make a very effective picture, especially with a little warm light breaking through in the foreground or hitting the center of interest. In a fog scene, you can't see the horizon line; it's lost. In your painting, you have an opportunity to make a striking pattern of your foreground and middle distance against a simple light gray background. You can paint the foreground in full value but, owing to the density of the atmosphere, objects should be rapidly grayed up the farther away they are in the picture. At a short distance, they should only be visible as simple spots of light and shade with practically no detail. Still farther away they should vanish completely.

A fog scene can be painted in tones of warm gray with a strong color in the foreground and center of interest. There will be a diffused down light on everything in the picture which will emphasize the horizontal top planes of objects in

MORNING LIGHT   In this picture, I was interested in the movement of the foreground wave as it surged over and around the nearby rocks. I find when I'm painting in the late morning or middle of the day, that there's a nice back lighting on the scene as I look toward the sun. This effect makes the scene most interesting to paint. In this picture, the upright planes are in shadow, while the more horizontal ones catch the light of the sun.

contrast to the darker upright planes. In painting a down light on a scene, it may help just to *think* of the light as a thin layer of snow on top of everything.

A rainy day scene makes a good picture, although it isn't quite as pleasant to look at as a fog scene. You have the same down light on everything from the sky, but you also get reflections in all smooth, wet, horizontal surfaces of light and dark objects directly above them. The tops of objects look wetter and are lighter. There are also darker clouds in the sky with very soft lower edges where the rain is falling. The whole picture can be painted in a cool color scheme.

STORM SCENES

A storm is always exciting and dramatic and can make a powerful picture. It will probably have to be done from memory, because it's no cinch to try to paint outside in bad weather. I've known a few hardy marine painters who used to try to paint outside in a howling gale and I occasionally ventured out myself in my younger days, but now I'm content to study the scene from as comfortable a spot as possible—usually from a cozy station wagon.

A stormy harbor hasn't quite the drama of a surf scene, but it can be very striking with a dark ominous sky reflected in the dark color of the harbor.

When you paint a stormy seascape, you can really have fun. Here again, it's generally impossible to make more than a few brief notes out by the sea. About all one can do is to study the storm scene and then try to paint it later in the studio under more peaceful conditions. It's sometimes possible to make pencil notes on the color or general action of the waves to help you remember the scene.

When painting any seascape, the nearer you can get to the level of the water the better, particularly in a storm scene when the oncoming waves loom up higher and higher against the sky as they draw near. A great wave rushing toward you is menacing and terrifying and adds greatly to the drama that we're trying to portray.

You can dramatize the sky by painting storm clouds even darker than you see them; also try suggesting wind and movement by the twisted shapes of the cloud formations.

In a real storm, there's generally a solid mass of foam close in to the rocks with no spots of clear water visible. After each wave comes crashing up over them, the rocks are dark and wet from the pouring sheets of water. When a wave strikes a rock, there's generally a great burst of foam and spray. It would be well to save this violent action for your center of interest. There's generally a heavy backwash as the water pours off the rocks and is pulled back out to sea to meet the next oncoming wave.

138

Storm scenes are often quite popular with some of our present-day juries of selection who will accept them for their shows and throw out some of the pictures of the more peaceful aspects of nature.

Possible picture buyers, on the other hand, may admire storm scenes, but they are more likely to buy a picture that is more tranquil—one that makes them feel happy when they look at it. So most artists paint two kinds of pictures—dark, gloomy ones that they hope the juries and art critics will like and pleasant, nostalgic scenes that are pleasant to look at and to live with which they hope will sell. Honestly, it's a great life!

RESTLESS SEA *The upright planes in the picture are in shadow while the strongest light hits on the horizontal planes.*

COCO HEAD   *The surf in the Hawaiian islands is always spectacular. Coco Head in the background is the next promontory after Diamond Head as you go east from Honolulu. Usually, the flat rocks on the beach are dotted with fishermen. They seem to fish away contentedly all day long, but I have yet to see them catch anything. The brilliant yellow sky was reflected in the shallow water in the foreground. The distant hills were gray lavender as were the clouds and the foam in shadow.*

17. Ships at Sea and Along the Coast

Boats, as I have mentioned previously, can be divided roughly into two classes—the small ones that operate off a beach or in harbors and the larger seagoing ones. So far, in this book, when I've talked about harbors, I've been thinking of the smaller harbors along the coast that are filled with rowboats, outboards, regular powerboats, pleasure and fishing boats. The waterfront scenery is on a small scale, usually with quaint old fishhouses and shacks scattered around just waiting to be put in a picture.

LARGE HARBORS

The larger harbors, however, are much more impressive, and everything is on a larger scale. You can find large freighters, beautiful ocean liners, an occasional naval vessel looking sleek and gray, old, battered tramp steamers, as well as countless tugs, barges, and powerboats. The wharfs are longer and in better repair, and the warehouses and other buildings on them are enormous. Back of the wharfs the buildings of the city loom in an impressive skyline. There's an effect of movement and excitement in the scene in striking contrast to the peaceful quiet of the small harbor, which often looks half-deserted. Yet, there is the same smell of the sea, and gentle lap of the water against the piles, and the cries of sea gulls that are typical of harbors everywhere. In rain or fog they appeal to your imagination, seem to be part of a different world, perhaps a simpler, pleasanter kind of life. If you love the sea, you can never forget it and will always be happiest when you get back to the coast and breathe the salty, fishy harbor air again.

SHIPS AT SEA

Painting ships at sea is a different problem. Here you have to imagine the scene or use sketches or photographs that you have made while on an ocean voyage. This type of picture depends for its effectiveness on the mood and light effect of the scene or on a dramatic story involving the age-old struggle of men against the sea. Ships sailing at sea have more pictorial interest when something is about to happen or is happening to them. Sinking ships, rescues, castaways on rafts, a ship struggling in heavy seas, all make more dramatic pictures.

BOATS ALONG THE COAST

Nearer the coast, you'll have smaller vessels, small freighters, and fishing boats and can show a distant headland for added interest. Along the shore, wrecks and old hulks are ideal subjects for pictures. I've always been fascinated by them

MACKEREL BOATS **The back lighting in this picture of the fishing boats along the Monhegan shore helps to dramatize the scene. I painted this from a pencil sketch that I had made at the shore. Collection, Mr. and Mrs. Roscoe C. Ingalls.**

QUIET COVE   *This view of the harbor was painted from the top of a sea wall, looking down on the boats in the foreground. The high eye line or horizon line eliminated most of the sky.*

and I'm sure that everyone likes to explore an old hulk on a beach and wonder how she came to be wrecked and what happened to the crew.

Let's look at some of the small boats that you encounter in a harbor or along the beaches and then take a look at some of the larger seagoing ships. Dinghies, skiffs, and dories are all rowboats, made for utility and service rather than for beauty. They're useful for short jaunts on the water when a powerboat isn't needed. There are also a great many outboard motorboats in use around the harbors. They get you places with speed and noise, and it's certainly easier to sit and ride than to have to do the rowing yourself.

Nowadays practically everyone who is anyone has an outboard motorboat moored in his backyard. It's become a status symbol. What some of the amateur sailors do when they go to sea, however, has to be seen to be believed.

Lobster boats are sturdy powerboats with a low cabin forward and a partially enclosed pilothouse and a large cockpit aft. Sometimes they're even simpler, ordinary motorboats with a tarpaulin over the fore part of the cockpit which helps protect the helmsman from the weather.

Fishing boats come in all sizes, from the small dragger with one hoist for nets to a large, powerful seagoing trawler that can spend weeks at sea and ride out any gale. There are all types of tugs, from small harbor tugs to large, powerful seagoing ones. Most tugs seem to be either in a hurry or to be towing several unwieldy barges behind them at a more decorous speed. There are countless freight and cargo vessels, from rusty old tramp steamers to fine, fast, modern freighters that compare favorably in comfort and style with the more *de luxe* ocean liners.

There is, in addition, every kind of small passenger-carrying motorboat and, of course, countless pleasure craft that vary in size from the tiniest class sailboat that will capsize at the drop of a hat to the plush, elegant yacht.

A BOAT OF MY OWN

I've always wanted to own a small, sturdy boat in which I could cruise around for part of the year. So far, there's been one slight obstacle to my acquiring the ideal craft; I have discovered, when talking about the kind of boat that I would like to own with my Gentle Wife, that her idea of the perfect boat is a nice, wide houseboat, preferably one with windowboxes filled with geraniums. This seems such a horrible idea to me that I guess I'll have to pass up the joys of being a boat owner for a while and content myself by looking at and painting them from a distance.

In the illustrations, I've pictured a few of the more familiar types of boats often seen along the coast.

ISLAND HARBOR   *This is another view of the harbor at Monhegan Island, Maine, and shows how effective back lighting can be when it's reflected on the quiet water of a harbor.*

18. Some Favorite Harbors

In recent years, we've lived mostly in New England, so quite a good deal of my harbor scenes are painted along the North Atlantic coast of the United States. For about four months of each year we live at Rockport, Massachusetts, where we give weekly painting demonstrations and operate the Ballinger Gallery. In my free time, I often paint around Rockport and the nearby harbors on Cape Ann.

NEW ENGLAND HARBORS

Rockport has a tiny harbor, just large enough for lobster boats and small yachts, and it does have the famous red fishhouse on the stone pier, painted so many times that it's widely known as Motif No. 1. If ever you're approaching insolvency and the bill collector is catching up with you, just paint a picture of this motif; it's as good as money in the bank, for you can practically always sell it. The only trouble is that after you've done it a number of times, it's extremely hard to think up different angles from which to paint, and you get so bored that you begin to wish you never had to see the picturesque old shack again.

Gloucester, on the other hand, is a busy seaport town with fishing boats coming in daily to supply the fish-processing plants around the harbor. There are dozens of boats to paint and many picturesque old wharfs and warehouses around the shore.

Some of the nearby harbors—Marblehead, Pigeon Cove, Lanesville and Annisquam—are picturesque but are mainly harbors for yachts or lobster boats.

When I go up to Monhegan Island, off the coast of Maine, each spring to paint the surf along its forbidding seaward side, I usually end up by painting its small harbor with the towering bulk of Manana, the adjoining island across the harbor. It makes a dramatic picture, particularly if painted in the afternoon with the sun behind it silhouetting it against the sky.

CITY HARBORS

New York City has a fine harbor, and you can find paintable subjects on either side of Manhattan Island. Both the Hudson and the East River views are good, and the view coming up the bay, with the Battery in the background, is magnificent.

Of course, San Francisco has a wonderful harbor and is exciting to paint, particularly the view of the Golden Gate at sunset or when the fog is coming in, turning the bay into a ghostly, mysterious no man's land.

SPRING AT LANE'S COVE   This small harbor on Cape Ann is most paintable from all directions. This view was painted from the sea wall looking toward the shore. The picture of the green boat in color was a view from the same spot, looking along the sea wall toward the harbor entrance. Collection, Mr. and Mrs. Ernest R. Lavigne.

In South America, the harbor of Rio de Janeiro is a spectacular sight but it's difficult to paint.

EUROPEAN AND CARIBBEAN PORTS

I remember a few spots in Europe with pleasure—several channel ports in England and Concarneau and Quimper in Brittany. I myself still prefer the smaller, more intimate harbors, although the large ones are certainly impressive.

In the Caribbean, I enjoy painting in the Virgin Islands, particularly the beautiful harbor of Charlotte Amalie at St. Thomas or Christiansted at St. Croix. One thing about painting near the equator is that there's practically no tide and your boats stay put a lot better than they do in the North, where they go up and down like elevators during the course of a day.

In the Caribbean and remote parts of the tropics, you can still see sailing craft that are working boats. Some are fishing boats, while others carry cargo between the different islands, providing a pleasant but cramped home for their numerous crew members when away from home. I've watched them coming and going in the small harbor of Christiansted on the island of St. Croix. The captains handle their sturdy craft with the precision and grace of any yachtsman. The boats are small sloops and schooners with rather blunt-looking hulls that are very solidly built. The sloops have their single masts nearer the middle of the boat than do our boats up north. Their mainsails have a long boom that projects well past the stern. This probably adds to the maneuverability of the craft and allows room at the bow for a couple of good-sized jibs. Their decks are filled with the usual assortment of gear lying around in seeming confusion. On deck there's often a fascinating collection of livestock—chickens, cows, dogs, and goats—that are quite at home aboard ship. One time on a boat from Trinidad, I saw a fat and very contented black pig. When I inquired if he was carried along for food, the captain said indignantly, "Certainly not!" The pig was the mascot and friend and they would not think of eating him. It sounded like a pleasant life for me; I almost felt like trading places with that pet pig!

At the stern of the larger boats there are often, on deck, two long box-shaped bunks with sliding doors for the captain and mate. When these boats are in port, a large tarpaulin stretched over the boom at the stern provides shade from the sun. Some of the larger boats have auxiliary power which is sometimes used when coming in or going out of the harbor, but most of the smaller ones are solely dependent on their sails for locomotion.

There are usually a number of American yachts in these waters and they're inclined to be trimmer and more gracefully built. However, I believe that if you were at sea in bad weather you'd be much safer in one of the native boats than in one of the beautiful but fragile modern yachts.

150

DECORATIVE ADDITIONS

Sailing vessels make such a fine decorative spot in a picture that I wish there were more around. Sails, when silhouetted against the sky, have fine pictorial possibilities and are equally effective in full light against a dark headland or sky.

When painting a harbor scene, I always add a sailboat if I possibly can. The sails are such a pleasant contrast to the skeleton-like appearance of the masts and rigging of the powerboats.

GOLDEN GATE *San Francisco is like no other spot on earth. It's my favorite city.*

RAMEA, NEWFOUNDLAND When I visited the island of Ramea off the Newfoundland coast last fall, I was fascinated by its small harbor and the many fishing boats anchored there. I tried sketching the harbor from the high rock you see in the background, but I found the view too panoramic with no real center of interest. I finally painted the scene from the other side of the harbor, looking across toward the fish processing plant with Man Of War Hill in the background.

Occasionally, you'll see a small sail on some of the draggers and lobster boats. These are simply to steady the boat at sea and are of little help in propelling it. However, in a picture, they do help to fill up the empty spaces around the masts. Nets hauled up to the masthead to dry also have good pictorial possibilities.

Last fall we spent three weeks visiting our good friends, Margaret and Spence Lake, in Newfoundland, a very paintable territory. The rugged cliffs and bays reminded me very much of the fjords of Norway. The scenery had a stark dramatic quality that fascinated me. Our hosts' hospitality during our visit was on the same grand style as the scenery, in fact we found on our return that it was difficult after all the excitement of our trip to adjust to the rather quiet, bucolic life that we lead here at home in Connecticut.

THE SURVIVORS *Scenes of peril at sea have always had a strange fascination for me,
and I frequently paint them. Collection, New Britain Art Museum.*

19. On the Spot Painting and Studio Work

Most serious artists today want to paint a picture that is more than a competent reproduction of a particular place or incident. They want to paint a more personal interpretation of the scene, one that has mood and feeling.

INTERPRETING THE SCENE

It may seem strange, but more fine pictures have been painted in the studio than have been painted directly from nature. When you're away from a scene you remember its mood, perhaps the dramatic lighting or color harmony and the general composition of the picture. In the studio you can paint it as you remember it and, free from distraction, you can concentrate on the important elements of the picture, leaving out all the unessentials. You can be more imaginative and creative in your color harmony and in your composition. However, in order to paint in this way you must be thoroughly familiar with the appearance of those things you want to include in your painting. The only way to gain this familiarity is to sketch and paint outdoors, directly from nature.

When you're outside painting—perhaps boats in a harbor or part of a seacoast—it's a good plan to paint the scene exactly as it looks to you. You want to know as much about it as possible, and the best way to gain this knowledge is to try to paint exactly what you see. A painter should do as much outdoor work as possible to keep him from getting stale. I think most of us find that, after painting in the studio all winter, we can hardly wait to get out and start painting the real thing again. You can get into some bad painting habits if you stay away too long from nature which, after all, should be your main source of inspiration.

In the case of the amateur or part-time painter whose opportunity to paint is limited, it may be necessary to do more indoor work. But whenever you have any spare time on weekends, after work, and on holidays, try to get outside and draw and paint as much as possible. You'll find it rewarding in many ways. In my own case, I find that while I spend considerable time painting in my studio, my outdoor sketches are invaluable reference material. And I know that I'd get into an awful rut if I stopped all outdoor work.

USING COLOR SCHEMES

When working in the studio, you can achieve some very interesting results by using an arbitrary color scheme. Some of the most effective pictures are those painted with a limited color scheme. For example, you can paint a monochro-

TRANQUIL HARBOR *The harbor at Stonington, Connecticut, gave me the idea for this picture. It isn't an entirely literal copy of the scene, but at least the rig of the fishing boats is typical of that part of the coast. I tried to suggest the peaceful mood of the scene without putting in a lot of photographic details. Collection, Mr. and Mrs. Spencer Lake.*

matic harmony using different values and tints of a single color. When I use one color throughout a picture, I sometimes add a bright accent of a closely related color. In *The Outer Reef,* I painted the whole picture in tones of blue-green except for the light strip of sky just above the horizon. There I used a pale lemon yellow. A warm brown can also be used advantageously with a little touch of pale blue somewhere.

My favorite picture is one using an analogous color scheme, that is, several closely related colors. A picture painted in a warm scheme—warm green, pale yellow and perhaps an orangey brown—can be a beautiful color arrangement. One painted in cool colors—purples, blues and greens—is equally satisfying. I'm never happier than when I'm painting some familiar scene in an arbitrary scheme. It gives a fresh and different look and almost always produces a mood that could never be conveyed by painting the subject in its more familiar aspects.

MAKING ALTERATIONS

In addition to painting a more personal and perhaps more imaginative picture in the studio, you'll find that your outdoor work frequently requires adding some finishing touches in the studio. Often you'll need to make minor changes and readjustments either in color or in composition, for after you've worked steadily on a picture for a considerable time your eyes are tired and you cannot always see your mistakes. However, when you see it later on with a fresh eye in the studio, you're able to catch your mistakes and correct them.

The only danger in working on these outdoor pictures in the studio is that you may *overwork* them. I know that I have trouble in this respect. I often see so many things in my outdoor sketch that I don't like that I repaint the whole picture in the studio creating an entirely different picture. So, try to repair only the more obvious mistakes and leave the rest of the picture alone. A painting, to be good, doesn't have to be a perfect picture. Sometimes a few sloppy touches add effectiveness to the whole composition. Anyway, let me repeat, try not to lose the vigor and freshness of your outdoor picture by polishing it too much in the studio.

WITHOUT DISTRACTION

One reason it's possible to be more creative while working in the studio is that there are fewer distractions. The weather doesn't bother you and the "friendly" bystanders with their fascinating comments aren't around. Some of my students say that they feel self-conscious, when painting outside, to have people stop and watch them. I think that the only thing to do is to relax and remember that the bystander probably can't draw or paint as well as you can.

I remember one cold, nasty winter day when I was painting a snow scene near my home in New Hartford, Connecticut. I was down in Maple Hollow trying to paint a view looking up a ravine. Every little while it would start to sleet or a puff of wind would blow my easel over. I tied the easel to a fence post and kept mopping the snow off the palette. My feet were wet; I was cold; I began to suspect that I was getting pneumonia. While I struggled with the elements and my picture, one of my neighbors came along. He was a sturdy old boy who looked hale and hearty—also warm and dry. He stopped and silently watched me paint for quite a while; then, when he finally decided to move on, he turned and said, "Well, it helps pass the time, don't it?"

THE LOST DORY *I never knew the story of this abandoned dory washed ashore on a lonely beach.*

TOLL OF THE SEA   *This was a wrecked fishing vessel on a distant shore.*

20. Practice Subjects

In this chapter, ten different compositions of surf and harbor scenes are presented for your use in practice painting. Each painting has a simple two-toned arrangement of light and dark and you can work out your own gradations of tone and color harmony.

I have suggested a possible treatment for each picture, but you'll want to try out your own ideas on some of the compositions.

You'll find that you can produce a variety of paintings by simply changing the color scheme, the direction of light or the mood of the paintings. It's a fine idea to use your own imagination as much as possible, for this is the way to paint a more creative and original type of picture.

PRACTICE SUBJECT I *In the first composition of surf breaking on a rocky shore, you might use a warm light on your cresting wave in the center of the picture; perhaps some clouds in the sky. You could use a little of the color scheme of the step-by-step demonstration picture of surf cresting on a rocky shore, though I would like to see you use a little more blue in the sky, in the foreground rocks, and in the surf in shadow. The floating foam in sunlight could be quite warm and a little darker in value than the foam of the big, cresting wave. You might use some pale blue-green in the sheet of water at the top of your big wave, and repeat it somewhere else in the picture where you have clear water in sunlight.*

In painting the sky, you could have some big, swelling clouds building up in the center, with patches of blue sky where I've used the gray tone. Remember that with a front or side light, your clouds are lighter and more brilliant overhead, but are grayer and cooler as they near the horizon. Because of this, you'll have to tone down the clouds as you work toward the middle of the picture. The distant wave in the center of the picture at the horizon is supposed to be in sunlight; it could be warmer and lighter than the rest of the sea around it.

PRACTICE SUBJECT II We have a sunset with a brilliant sky reflected in the quiet water of the harbor. The dark pattern consists of the dragger, with its reflections in the water, in the center; the boats tied up to the wharf on the left; the distant hill and the lobster boat on the right. You can paint the sky and the reflecting water different shades of orange, yellow, and pink; the clouds, warm grays with just a suggestion of blue or green near the top; the various darks could be warm browns, greens, and purples. Let the water in the foreground be a darker shade of brownish green. Keep a good bit of white in the light parts of the sky and in its reflection in the water. Don't show the sun itself; it lies hidden behind the hill.

PRACTICE SUBJECT III *In a surf on a sandy beach, you have the light coming from the right, bathing the whole picture with warmth. I'd suggest having pinkish clouds, some pink mixed through the blue sky, and a good deal of warmth in the cresting waves and the floating foam. The masses of foam that stand up above the surface of the water always catch more light and should be painted much higher in key than the horizontal portions of foam lying flat on the surface of the water. Be sure that the front edge of each of the flattened-out waves is considerably lighter than the trailing foam behind it.*

The distant sea could be a rich, dark blue-green with a little of the gray of the sky reflecting in it. The clear water of the large cresting waves could be a little more green than blue, and the clear water between the masses of floating foam a lighter shade of green; while the color of the shallow water close to shore would be more the color of the sandy beach beneath it. The wet sand next to the water is more of a brownish purple, while the dry sand farther up the beach is a grayish tan and lighter in value. The trailing, floating foam generally picks up a little lavender from the sky.

PRACTICE SUBJECT IV *Here's a fog scene with a simple down light on the float, on the men and the boats in the left foreground. The schooner in the distance will be just a flat gray silhouette with very little detail. Paint the sky and water a warm gray, a little lighter directly overhead in the center, a little darker and greener in the lower right hand corner. The lobster boat is a dark brownish green. The skiff next to the float is light gray with a red gasoline can in it. The dory next to it is orange-red. The man in the boat is wearing a red shirt. The deck and roof of the lobster boat should be orangey yellow. The man on the dock is wearing yellow overalls. The reflections in the water are the brownish greens. A cool down light is cast over the entire composition.*

PRACTICE SUBJECT V is an open sea picture which I think might be painted with the light coming from the right side. The upper clouds could be a warm dark note; under that, you could have a band of blue sky getting a little warmer as you approach the source of light on the right. The lower bank of clouds would be a pink gray, though a little light might hit on the upper part of this cloud bank. The distant water would be a blue gray while the clear water in the foreground would be a rich, dark blue-green. The swell in the lower left hand corner should be the darkest spot in the picture and could be a very dark blue-green. The clear water just above it with the floating foam could have a little more sky color in it and would not be quite as dark. The floating foam would be a warm cream color with perhaps a small amount of lavender added to it. It should be painted with your brush strokes following in the direction of the movement of the foam. The big cresting waves should be painted with up and down strokes to suggest weight and thickness. I would keep the foam of the breaking wave in the lower right hand corner toned down with only a little light along the top of it. It isn't a good idea to have too much contrast in a corner of the picture, because it takes away from your center of interest. The cresting wave in the center would be quite light, with a little cool shadow on the left side of the foam masses. You will see how to model the foam of your big cresting wave by studying the color reproduction of the open sea demonstration picture.

165

PRACTICE SUBJECT VI   In this twilight view of Motif Number 1, try to paint the whole picture in two values. The light sky and its reflection in the water would be a pale orange. The buildings, draggers, and dark reflections in the water would be brown, blue, and green, with just a touch of grayed-up red in the motif itself. The draggers would probably have green hulls and pale greenish brown deckhouses. The dory could be dull orange, also a couple of the lobster buoys in the left foreground. I took the liberty of putting some fishing gear, a lobster pot and the markers on the end of T-Wharf in the foreground. I never saw any there, but let's pretend that someone left them there momentarily. I think we need a little interest in the foreground, don't you?

PRACTICE SUBJECT VII is a moonlight scene with surf breaking on the rocky Monhegan coast. It should be painted in rich tones of rather grayed-up blue-green with a good bit of warmth through the whole picture. Contrary to the usual belief, a moonlight scene isn't just a picture painted in cold greens and blues; it really has a lot of warmth in it, particularly in the shadows.

I'd suggest that you have the moon just above the upper edge of the picture, but paint the upper clouds a pale grayish pink as though the moon were shining through them. This will enable you to have your brilliant moonlight reflected on the sea and on your foreground surf. You can have just a little warmth in the moonlight reflecting on the water.

The sea can be a shade darker than the sky, but be sure to have very soft edges at the horizon line. These soft edges will make the path of light reflecting on the water all the more brilliant and sparkling. The front planes of the cresting wave should be a grayed-up blue-green with very little detail or modeling in them. In moonlight, there's very little detail to be seen in the shadows. You can get them in the right shape and general value, but keep them just simple flat spots of tone.

I would try to lose as many edges as possible throughout the picture, only accenting the spots where the moonlight really hits. The foreground rocks in shadow should be a dark brownish blue, with a suggestion of warmth in the top planes that catch the light. The great charm of a moonlight scene is in its illusive air of mystery, so be sure that you don't whittle everything out in too much detail.

PRACTICE SUBJECT VIII *In this view of New York Harbor, paint the scene with a warm pinkish gray sky and water. Paint the tug in the right hand corner a warm brown and its cabin and pilothouse orange-red. The hulls of the big freighter and passenger boat on the left can be warm brown and the superstructure light cream. The smokestacks on the freighter could be red with a dark band at the top. Pale tan-colored smoke can pour from the freighter's funnel. Keep the sky line of lower Manhattan a very pale, warm, bluish gray—a flat silhouette with no detail. This will suggest haze and fog in the distance and will be a lot easier than putting in every painful detail of the skyscrapers.*

168

PRACTICE SUBJECT IX   This is a fog scene and should be painted in tones of a warm gray. The horizon line should be lost and the masses of white foam in the distance should be just flat patterns of light, with hardly any detail and with very soft edges. You have a diffused down light on everything in the picture, with all of your upright planes a little darker than the horizontal ones.

If you paint your foreground rocks just as strong and dark as possible, you'll be able to produce the effect of fog by painting everything in the background much grayer and softer.

The nearby surf and floating foam can be painted with plenty of detail to contrast with the half-lost shapes of the more distant waves. In the sky, you can suggest fog by having the sky a little lighter at the top of the picture and having a few soft swirls of a slightly darker tone here and there in the sky.

PRACTICE SUBJECT X *We have a marine scene in the moonlight. Sky and water are a warm purplish blue with a little green. Both the dark schooner and reflections are dark purplish brown. The distant shore and boat are bluish purple. The piles in the right foreground are brownish purple. Clouds near the moon are rather warm tan. The light of the moon on the clouds and on the water is a pale yellow with lots of white in it. There's just a touch of warmer yellow in the reflections of the moonlight in the water at the bottom of the picture.*

Conclusion

I've always thought that marine painters were the luckiest people, because they are painting the most magnificent subject in the world. However, you have to be really fond of the sea to go to all the trouble of learning to paint it. Boats and harbors are equally fascinating and require both knowledge and skill to do them justice. Probably the average person gets just as much pleasure from looking at a harbor scene as he does from a surf or open sea painting.

THREE THINGS TO PRACTICE

At the risk of seeming to be repetitious, I'd like to restate briefly that the three important elements in a picture are composition, good drawing, and color. If you wish to improve your own work, you should learn everything that you can about drawing, color, and composition and should paint just as much as possible. After all, the only way that you can learn to paint is to work at it constantly.

Good drawing is the foundation of any picture and should never be neglected. I've spent my whole life attempting to learn to draw with more facility and accuracy and have never been entirely satisfied with the results. You can never draw too well, so try and improve your drawing by always carrying a sketchbook with you wherever you go and by making brief sketches of everything that interests you. In other words, just try and draw everything everywhere. After all, when you're painting a picture, you're constantly drawing with your brush, so you're really always drawing when you're painting.

Your color, too, will improve with practice and you'll be able to get nicer color harmony in all your pictures. As you gain experience, you'll learn what colors look well together and you will be able to use them with good taste.

Composition, or design, is the most important part of your picture, so always try to get the most effective design that you can in your painting. When you go to an exhibition, make a note of the dark and light pattern of any of the pictures that appeal to you. When outdoors, study any interesting subject that meets your eye and see if you can figure out its basic design—its linear structure as well as its dark and light pattern. All this takes hard work and concentration but it's worth the effort to be able to paint a fine picture—one that will please your family and startle your friends.

Originality is a great thing to strive for and I think it's a good idea to avoid imitating another artist's work, even if you like his style and know that his pictures are very saleable.

STUDYING OTHER PAINTERS

It's a better plan to study the work of all of the marine painters, either at exhibitions or through reproductions of their paintings. You can get a great many ideas from their work that will help your own pictures. When you're influenced by the work of a number of artists, your painting won't resemble the work of any one painter, and will look entirely original.

When you're viewing the work of other artists, try to look for the good points in their pictures. Never pay much attention to the faults. It's only the faults in your own pictures that matter. None of us are perfect painters, and I think it's easy to see faults in some of the finest works ever painted. Pictures are like friends. You like them in spite of their faults. So if there are a few spots in a picture that are less than perfect, think nothing of it as long as the general effect is good.

DEVELOPING YOUR OWN STYLE

As regards your individual style and technique, you'll find that if you paint in the manner and style that is most natural to you, you'll begin to develop certain characteristic mannerisms that will distinguish your pictures from the work of everyone else.

Probably a number of you folks are like myself and can spend only a portion of the year at the seashore. In that case, when painting away from the water, you have to use as material either sketches you made at the shore or photographs of surf scenes. It's better to work from a black-and-white photograph than to copy someone else's painting. When you only copy another artist's picture you don't have to use your imagination, and consequently are not learning as much as when you're working out something original.

IT'S HARD WORK

I've often been asked if I thought a person had to be born with a great talent in order to be a good painter. I don't think this is so, nor that you have to be a genius to paint a creditable picture. Most people who have a desire to paint have some artistic talent, as a person rarely wants to do something for which he has no aptitude. If you have ordinary common sense, good taste, and the ability to work hard enough to learn the fundamentals of painting, you'll be able to paint a picture. When you're painting, you're training your eye and hand to see and record the scene before you. There's nothing that can take the place of hard work. The only way to learn to paint is to constantly paint.

I've tried to include in this book all of the ideas on marine painting that I thought might be of help to the average painter. There's so much to learn about painting the surf and shore that I've always felt one lifetime wasn't long enough to learn all about it. I hope that this book will help the reader to avoid some of the long frustrating hours that I've had to spend in learning about marine painting, the hard way. Perhaps some day, if I'm lucky, I may meet some of you nice people when we're both painting out on the shore or around the waterfront and you can tell me how you are making out painting surf and shore. Until then, good-bye and good luck!

172

SPINDRIFT *My Gentle Wife objects to my painting so many pictures of wrecks. She says that they depress her and the heavy seas make her feel slightly seasick. I hope that they don't have this effect on the general public. My reason for painting them isn't to annoy her, as she suspects, but because I think they often make an exciting and dramatic picture. I tried to roughly suggest the figures on the rocks without really drawing them in at all.*

Index

174

New Edition Edited by Susan E. Meyer

Design Adapted by Wm. Harris

Photographs of paintings by Irving Blomstrann

Composed in Eleven Point Baskerville by Atlantic Linotype Company, Inc.

Offset by The Haddon Craftsmen, Inc.

Bound by The Haddon Craftsmen, Inc.